LEARN EMBEDDED SYSTEM WITH STM32

Building an RTOS Programming for
Embedded Systems Building an NEC
Decoder with STM32 and C on Cortex-M4

BY

Nishimoto Takehiko

TABLE OF CONTENTS

4

ST-LINK SOFTWARE INSTALLATION

High in this section, still in software installation in the Linux operating system will be covered. We still think they still receive five volt power from a USB port. The civil war by the interface can be disconnected from the target by removing two jumpers. But the stealing software installation executed the following steps in a common line.

You have now installed software for this program and let's try to connect the dots, get them to see you on the discovery board.

GNU ARM TOOLCHAIN INSTALLATION

This section explains how to install the new Ottoman, but to change in the Linux operating system and why the new arm and the toolchain contains integrated unvalidated packages featuring the DC compiler and libraries used for the battered metal embedded software development. The toolchain targets 32 bit arm cortex, a cortex, R and cortex and based microprocessor devices. The toolchain is open source and supports different cortex processors.

GNU ARM Embedded Toolchain

- Cortex-M0, Cortex-M0+, Cortex-M1, Cortex-M3, Cortex-M4, Cortex-M7, Cortex-M23, Cortex-M33, Cortex-M55

- STM32F4VGT6 → Cortex-M4 CPU

We will not dive deeply into the microprocessor topic, but the critical thing to mention is that the Cortex and Protocell series represents our course's most considerable interest. The 32 bit arm cortex for microprocessor is used in and 32 a four digit six microcontroller on the discovery board. The manual installation is recommended to select a better future for the toolchain.

STM32F4DISCOVERY BOARD OVERVIEW

On the discovery board, two buttons are available, a user, a button, and then see a reset button on the external peripherals up and not the AC and three X's accelerometer and omnidirectional digital microphone or LCD and the USB on the go connector, the external MCU quartz crystal because I need my hands frequency the target MCU ASTM 32 F for 07 Vegeta six is connected to the string program of a two while serial debugging interface. The main MCU has such features one megabyte of memory, 192 kilobyte of RAM or text and for an arm processor running at up to one hundred sixty eight hertz frequency.

The main MCU features:

- 1 MByte of flash memory
- 192 kByte of RAM
- 168 MHz Cortex-M4 ARM CPU
- NVIC unit for interrupt processing
- GPIO ports with interrupt capabilities
- More than 12 timers
- 3 ADC, 1 DAC, 3 SPI, 3 I2C, 6 UART
- SDIO, Ethernet, and two USB interfaces
- RCC unit, two watchdog timers, a HW CRC unit

And we see unit or interrupt processing iReports with external interoperability is a comprehensive set of internal peripheral units. More than 12 counters predecease one DHC three, spy three I to see and six user interfaces is the IO Internet and to use be interfaces with Microcontroller has a hardware CRC unions watchdog, Timmers O.S.S. Union. Not all. But if all unions can be simultaneously used because they share the same input output, Beane's the MCU has the I give you one hundred cases.

IR RECEIVER AND LED CONNECTIONS

The Internet to see what was in Istanbul. You can use any infrared receiver of any kind, but the important thing is that it can receive a 38 kilohertz carrier frequency. The NSC remote control uses this frequency to transmit commands. And now we will connect an infrared receiver to the discovery that bought the receiver. Its purpose is to receive this from an infrared remote control and drive Szubin, which will be connected to it. I decided to choose a PC one pin to connect the infrared receiver output ping from the practical considerations and keep things as simple as possible. It's been out perfectly since the discovery bought by one male connected to provide the three volt power supply for the infrared receiver. This voltage is suitable for the receivers.

Regular operation rewards power supply and ground pins on the P1 connector, much the same infrared receiver power pins. Due to the above reasons I have decided to use A, B, C, one being. Eight ladies have been connected to the body and Bobby. Besides, the one word, LSD can be turned on and turned off if a specific infrared remote control government is received. We have just covered a hardware set up which will be used in this course. Now we are approaching the more interesting and exciting part of the course. In the next lecture of this course we will become more familiar with an NSC protocol which has a command format and remote control will be reported from the infrared receiver biological analyzer.

NEC PROTOCOL TIMING DIAGRAM ANALYSIS

We have approached an important part of, of course, the NSC protocol description and the protocol will define our firmware algorithm, which we are going to implement in the next four sections. Let's have a lo What are the main protocol features? Distance modulation. Both address and command are a bit logical. Zero takes one point twelve milliseconds to be transmitted logical, one takes two point twenty five minutes, second to be transmitted. After that, the repeat quote is being sent as long as the button is held. In this section, we will analyze the NSC protocol time diagram for this. I will recall the culture from the Internet received output data. Let's connect a logic analyzer to the ground and the MCU, one port boultbee. I will use the field channel, which corresponds to the orange color. The recorded data will contain a comment from a remote control.

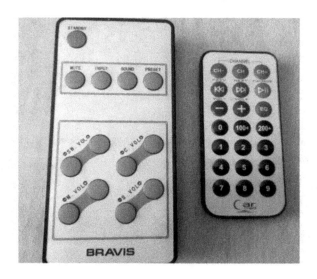

These are two remote controls which I will use in your remote control with the NSC protocol. At this point, it doesn't matter which sampling frequency for the logic analyzer is said. For this channel, The Logic analyzes, political decoder has been configured for comment analyses.

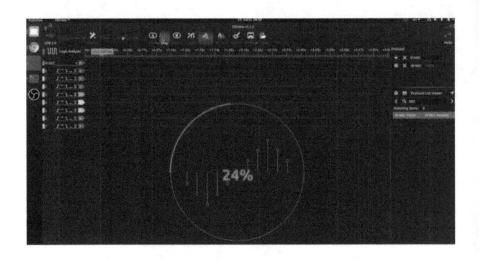

I press a start button and the logic analyzer starts to record. Just after this, I press and hold for a second or one of the buttons on the remote control. Then they do the same with a few other buttons. Now, Channel three should contain the timing diagram, which has been recorded. The infrared receiver output active signal level is low, which means that when a remote control transmits at greater frequency, the infrared receiver's output is zero. The first pulse is a nine millisecond HCG pulse, which was used for the infrared receiver synchronization. Then the path is followed by a long four and a half millisecond both. As we see, there can be a relatively small difference between the NSC protocol description and the timing diagram, which is recorded from the remote control.

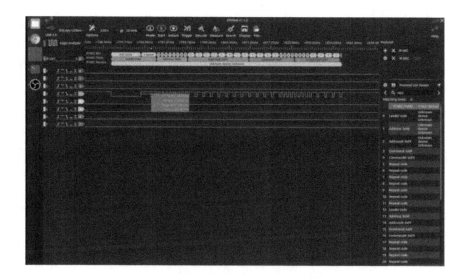

The next eight bits are the system address, followed by the eight bit inverted system address. As we know, a system address corresponds to a specific device type. Finally, they did command and it's a bit of inversion of transmitted after the system address. A stock bid which is followed by the inverted command data field, as it turns out, although the NSC protocol defines a length of five hundred sixty microseconds for each data pulse, the pulse's actual length might have a difference of 10-15 percent. In our case, this real world feature will be handled far away so that we should not worry about it. When a button on the remote control is pressed, the command is transmitted only once. After that, the rapid growth is being sent as long as the button is held. The repeat could consist of a nine millisecond HCG pulse, followed by a short two point twenty five millisecond pause and the five hundred sixty microseconds stop it. In every NSC command, the agency policies are spaced in a way that the time between two of them in the front end is 108 millisecond. 108 millisecond time separation applies to both command and repeating court fields in any SI protocol. Now we understand how comments in the protocol unfolded before we can start to implement and infer where we should initialize our system peripherals.

STM32 PERIPHERALS INITIALIZATION

We had a brief overview of the NSC protocol. Now we need to initialize our system peripherals. This will be just a few things, but they all are essential. First, we need to define which system we want to use and configure it in our system. The second step is to initialize input and output. GPI Europeans connected to the infrared receiver and the ladies. This step also defines how the MCU will handle the signal edges and the infrared receiver output data in the next will be to select the timer, which is used to measure time intervals in the system, such as bit length and pauses.

The important thing is to configure the MCU in such a way that the critical system events are handled automatically. For this reason, the system interrupts will be used. ASTM 32, Cuba makes two will be used during this section. I will export a project which will be used as a template for the NSC coding algorithm implementation. It's possible to configure the storm team to peripherals manually by writing code, but with the storm Cuba, Max, we can do this much faster. However, we still will need to do some modifications manually. In addition, it's much more convenient to see C-code to understand the initialization procedure better.

SYSTEM CLOCK CONFIGURATION

Along with this I will introduce how to configure the FCC reset and flood control unit. Before we start selecting frequency, let's tell our tool that the external quartz crystal will be used. Now, in their six year window, we see that there are several system sources. An internal LCAC, later, external quartz crystal and a pillow. For the discovery MCU by default, the internal 16 Ursy oscillator is enabled; we can specify the external quartz crystal frequency from four to 26 megahertz. On the discovery board her squad is used. In our case, the frequency is enough for the NSC protocol decoding purposes, but let's make the look frequency higher. And to do this, the external world crystal, together with the PLL bloc, will be used, the eight Muirhead's crystal frequency will be used as an input for the PLO. Let's assume that a 60 former health system look frequency is needed. Well, this thing put eight missiles, frequency is divided by four before it arrives and the PLO input. Then it's multiplied by 64 and divided by two.

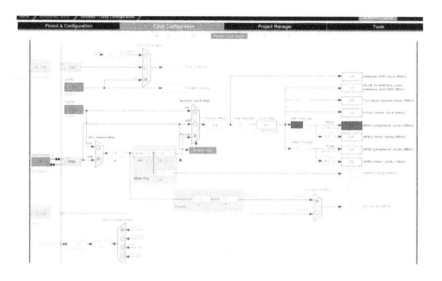

Now a 64 megahertz frequency is a system called clock frequency. Unlike the core, the storm, 32 system peripherals cannot run at the maximum frequency. For example, although the maximum C.P.U frequency can be configured as high as 168 and then see you peripherals and the work at up to 84, up to 40 tubular hills only depending on which bus and peripherals are used. That is why we should divide sixty four megahertz by two to get attached to a health frequency for the PCL came one bass. Now, there are no clear conflicts in the current global reconfiguration and it can be used in our firmware. The clock frequency does not have a substantial impact on the G.P.A. operation. Still, it does affect the timing scalar value, which defines by which number the peripheral input frequency must be divided to obtain the desired time intervals, measurement, and accuracy. We will consider this in the time initialization section of this course. So far we have configured the system core and peripheral devices called frequencies. You can configure your coquetry with the desired frequencies and practice on their unit various configurations in the next section in your configuration for the discovery of what will be considered.

GPIO CONFIGURATION

This section covers the GPA, your configuration for the microcontroller on the College Board, the GPA, your purpose is to interface the microcontroller with the real world for mutual interaction. In our particular case, the infrared receiver and LCD are connected to the controller input and output, respectively. The GPA, your business direction defines where they've been reached, the logical signal level or drives the external load. That means that each of the GPA Europeans basically can work as an input or an output. In fact, in the SDM 32 microcontroller family, there are more than two possible configuration modes. The output and alternate configuration modes are low, the additional configuration option as the Push-Pull or open drain transistors stage. Besides, the output, altitude and input modes may have or may not have enabled pull up or pull down resistors, such a variety of Gevalia configuration modes selects the best application capabilities. An ABC report keeping one connected to the

Internet receiver's output pin is configured as an input with a pull up resistor enabled. Although the receiver has a built in pull up resistor on the data pin, the pull up register in the supercheap in one is enabled. Also, the infrared receivers, MCU Upin, need to have the rising and falling edge trigger detection, you might think. What it gives to us. The answer is simple, having the GPA, your external configure, it allows them, you forget to call an external interrupt function. And whenever the infrared receiver output data changes its logical level, this makes the big time and pauses interval measurement more accurate and saves you time.

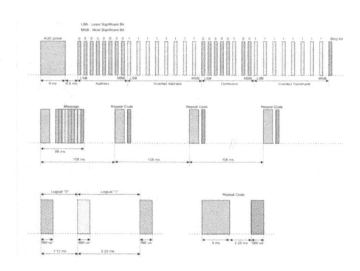

For the ladies, we need to initialize the G.P.A. as output, Push-Pull, in my case, I have an extra eight Leidy's connected to the Discovery Board. If you count from zero, the Pardeep from zero to four and six to seven work as output's for the corresponding LHD. The fifth bit, which activates the lady with the same number, comes from Polsby; such a decision has since been five conflicts with one of the on board external peripherals. Well, the four on board Discovery Leidy's, the board DPN from 12 to 15, also act in outwell Push-Pull G.P.A.. This Leidy's we might want to use. Now the system has the desired frequency and the GPA, your operating modes correspond to the external peripherals connections.

TIMER_S BASIC CONFIGURATION

They're used for time in interval measurement, the NSC decoder will require a single timer to measure the length of the pulses and pauses between them. It doesn't matter which time it is used and I will select Taimur three. In this case, the internal report will be used, but not on the stand, which peripheral boss is connected to Taimur three and what it's called frequency to find this out. Let's check them. See your datasheet. As it was mentioned in the previous LCAC initialization section, the peripherals' look frequency is important to note, select a valid time scalar value. If we open the reference manuals page where there is A, B, B, one peripheral clock and then register it, bits are described. We will see the timer three is enabled by this register and it corresponds to the APB one bus and is Bustelo rescaling. In the SDM, such as Turkey, Biomax threw in the FCC window, we can see that all the AP one part timers will get the 60 for health frequency, including Taimur three. Now returning to the timer initialization procedure defining scalars, well, we must know the EB one Busque lock frequency and the shortest time duration, which needs to be measured. In the NSC protocol, we have five hundred sixty microseconds, minimal pulse length. Let's assume that we would like to have a time measurement accuracy of 10 microseconds as the least time interval which we can measure with our timer, the frequency of 10 microseconds period is 100 kilohertz.

Timer Prescaler and Compare Values Calculation

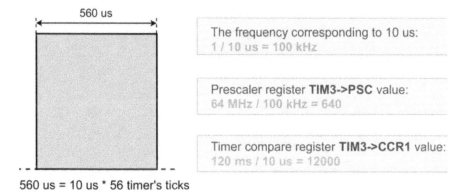

The frequency corresponding to 10 us:
1 / 10 us = 100 kHz

Prescaler register **TIM3->PSC** value:
64 MHz / 100 kHz = 640

Timer compare register **TIM3->CCR1** value:
120 ms / 10 us = 12000

560 us = 10 us * 56 timer's ticks

We might not need to have such high accuracy, but let's keep it at the moment. 640 is the time scalar value for the 64 megahertz health timer, low frequency to have a 10 microsecond time resolution. Let's use this scalar value during the timer three initialization. It's important to ensure that the system has returned to its initial state to be ready for a new government reception and decoding. Now we need to handle full situations when there are no policies received for more than 120 milliseconds. In simple words, assistant timeout is required, the best way of doing this is to use a timer, compare more to interrupt, which is triggered when the time comes in the register, which is a value stored in the output compare register for 120 milliseconds. Both a timer and compare value needs to be 12000. Due to the timeless complexity, some of the parameters need adjusting encode, this will help us to understand better how it works.

NESTED VECTORED INTERRUPT CONTROLLER INTRODUCTION

This section will explain how to enable interruptive globally and assign their priorities, unless that vector to interrupt controller or simply NYSE is in advanced interrupt controller for cortex and processors being closely coupled with an arm, buchel and Visi enables dynamic interrupt, prioritization and low latency interrupt handling the NYSE interrupts are pre-emptive. This means that an interrupt with the higher priority will be processed as fast as possible by a visi, even when an interrupt with a lower priority is already being handled. This means that the context of the interrupter with the lower priority will be pushed automatically to stack up on the high priority in Thrupp Trigorin. The low priority in the right context will be restored back when the high priority interrupts helping the protest. For our NSC protocol, decadent FairWear, interrupt priorities are not important for its integration into other projects. You might need to play with interrupt priorities a bit.

Now, we must enable the line one and time or three global interrupts in a stream. Bemax puts all the ticks as you see on the screen. I will assign the same priority seven for both interrupts. In the project management window, in advanced settings, change hardware, abstraction, layer to low level. In the toolchain, select Makefile. Stack and heap say this should not be changed, however, even if you change, it should not affect the industry, the code operation. Give a name to the project, select its location and the president red button. Now our template is ready. We will continue with the code writing in the next section.

MAKEFILE MODIFICATIONS FOR ST-LINK

This short lecture introduces the Makefile modification necessary for the simplified SDM that the two MCU fletching using a simple command is using as stealing as a physical interface. The Esteve command line tool flashes a user faraway binary file into the Maraba controller. The stiff left to write the binary file at the specific address in the controller flash memory, where the file will start its execution after the system reset. In the SDM, 32 microcontrollers, the flash memory starts at the address, eight and six years in the hexadecimal form, this government writes the binary at this address.

Let's store the comment in our makefile. To call this comment from a comment line, we should type make flesh and press enter. Another useful comment is for erasing the entire flash memory array as the flash arrays, if you are not certain about the flash memory content type, make arrays in the command line window.

PROJECT STRUCTURE AND FIRMWARE ALGORITHM

This section introduces a project for the structure and the description of the inner city code of our. The Saudi ambassador to Cuba, Max, generates a project template which has the following files, Mansi main page, and you see Iasi, NCAR, Page and Makefile and start up a similar file Ellinger script, a file with the Interop handlers, a system file containing the specific system functions and the steam to the to call and peripheral drivers. The NSCLC file contains the coder's functions they interrupt. Handlers have been moved to the NCAR see file to keep order and see the code. The logic in one place, the zip code library will not be covered in this course. The important peripheral drivers will be explained to a certain extent.

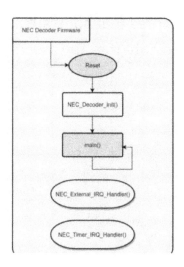

Now let's have a look at the firmware algorithm. At the top level, the firmware consists of several functions. Power on cycle or a hard reset causes the fire where to start its execution from this specific address in the MCU flash memory and this address, the interrupt vector stable is located. If we open and assemble, start up while we can see that the interactive vectors are grouped into sections, the first section contains the system exceptions. And the second one includes the system interrupts. The main difference between these two sections is that the exceptions relate to the armed cortex C.P.U core, whereas the interrupts are driven by the microcontroller peripherals. There is a tractor residing in the system, acceptable space, and the final word jumps to the place in the assembler file, which is marked as reset handler. And here is that pointer register is initialized. This government loads and underscores that constant into this checkpoint to register. Please note that the assembly language is not case sensitive.

```asm
43 /* start address for the .bss section. defined in linker script */
44 .word  _sbss
45 /* end address for the .bss section. defined in linker script */
46 .word  _ebss
47 /* stack used for SystemInit_ExtMemCtl; always internal RAM used */
48
49 /**
50  * @brief  This is the code that gets called when the processor first
51  *         starts execution following a reset event. Only the absolutely
52  *         necessary set is performed, after which the application
53  *         supplied main() routine is called.
54  * @param  None
55  * @retval : None
56 */
57
58     .section  .text.Reset_Handler
59   .weak   Reset_Handler
60   .type   Reset_Handler, %function
61 Reset_Handler:
62   ldr   sp, =_estack        /* set stack pointer */
63
64 /* Copy the data segment initializers from flash to SRAM */
65   movs  r1, #0
66   b  LoopCopyDataInit
67
68 CopyDataInit:
69   ldr  r3, =_sidata
70   ldr  r3, [r3, r1]
71   str  r3, [r0, r1]
72   adds  r1, r1, #4
73
74 LoopCopyDataInit:
75   ldr  r0, =_sdata
76   ldr  r3, =_edata
77   adds  r2, r0, r1
78   cmp  r2, r3
79   bcc  CopyDataInit
80   ldr  r2, =_sbss
81   b  LoopFillZerobss
82 /* Zero fill the bss segment. */
83 FillZerobss:
84   movs  r3, #0
85   str  r3, [r2], #4
86
87 LoopFillZerobss:
88   ldr  r3, = _ebss
89   cmp  r2, r3
90   bcc  FillZerobss
91
92 /* Call the clock system intirialization function.*/
93   bl  SystemInit
94 /* Call static constructors */
95     bl  __libc_init_array
96 /* Call the application's entry point.*/
97   bl  main
98   bx  lr
99 .size  Reset_Handler, .-Reset_Handler
```

You might have previously noticed that on this score is that constant is located before there is that vector in the exception stable. If you open a Lincoln script, you'll see that this constant value is 20 zero to four zeros in the hexadecimal form. This constant represents the REM address where the state is located. Then the phone calls the system and main functions. From the main function, Bauer calls the NSC the coordinate function, which initializes assistant Cloke iReports a hardware timer and interrupts. On this diagram, the energy I see controller initialization is shown separately, but in code, the GPO in its function contains the NYC logic for the X. I want to interrupt. And in the end, see time at it.

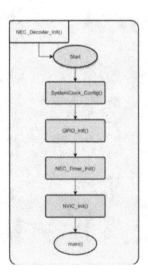

Function for the timer. Such a way of writing code helps to keep all the necessary interrupts, and they have been functions in one place or each peripheral. Then the main program jumps to the infinite while loop. Then you see the court in firmware includes interrupt handlers, the external interrupt handler and the time interrupt handler, the NSC decoding firmware is completely interop driven and is beneficial for its future integration into existing code. Besides, the interrupts can be assigned their priorities in the NSC irh while they interrupt.

```c
54   * Exported constants
55   */
56  // NEC Decoder TypeDefs
57  #define    IR_RECEIVER_PORT            GPIOC
58  #define    IR_RECEIVER_PIN             LL_GPIO_PIN_1
59  #define    IR_RECEIVER_LINE            LL_EXTI_LINE_1
60  #define    NEC_Timer                  TIM3
61  #define    RCC_APB_Periph_NEC_Timer   LL_APB1_GRP1_PERIPH_TIM3
62  #define    NEC_Timer_IRQ_Handler      TIM3_IRQHandler
63  #define    NEC_Timer_IRQn             TIM3_IRQn
64  #define    NEC_External_IRQ_Handler   EXTI1_IRQHandler
65  #define    NEC_EXTI_IRQn              EXTI1_IRQn
66
67  // NEC Decoder Constants
68  #define    SYSTEM                     0
69  #define    FAULT                      0xFF
70  #define    MAX_BITS                   32
71  #define    START_OF_INV_SYS           9
72  #define    START_OF_COM               17
73  #define    START_OF_INV_COM           25
74  #define    DECODE_IS_OK               0x55
75
76  #define        INPUT_TIM_FREQUENCY        64000000 // 64 MHz Timer Clock
77  #define        FREQ_10_US                 100000
78  #define        TIME_SLOT_US               10
79  #define    PULSE_LENGTH_US                560
80
81  #define    PRESCALER_10_US            (INPUT_TIM_FREQUENCY / FREQ_10_US)
82  #define    TIME_560_US                (PULSE_LENGTH_US / TIME_SLOT_US)
83  #define    DEV_560_US                 TIME_560_US / 4
84  #define    MIN_560_US                 (TIME_560_US - DEV_560_US)
85  #define    MAX_560_US                 (TIME_560_US + DEV_560_US)
86
87  #define    TIME_1_125_MS              (TIME_560_US * 2)
88  #define    DEV_1_125_MS               (TIME_1_125_MS / 8)
89  #define    MIN_1_125_MS               (TIME_1_125_MS - DEV_1_125_MS)
90  #define    MAX_1_125_MS               (TIME_1_125_MS + DEV_1_125_MS)
91
92  #define    TIME_2_25_MS               225
93  #define    DEV_2_25_MS                (TIME_2_25_MS / 8)
94  #define    MIN_2_25_MS                (TIME_2_25_MS - DEV_2_25_MS)
95  #define    MAX_2_25_MS                (TIME_2_25_MS + DEV_2_25_MS)
96
97  #define    TIME_4_5_MS                (TIME_2_25_MS * 2)
98  #define    DEV_4_5_MS                 (TIME_4_5_MS / 8)
99  #define    MIN_4_5_MS                 (TIME_4_5_MS - DEV_4_5_MS)
100 #define    MAX_4_5_MS                 (TIME_4_5_MS + DEV_4_5_MS)
101
102 #define    TIME_9_MS                  (TIME_4_5_MS * 2)
103 #define    DEV_9_MS                   (TIME_9_MS / 8)
104 #define    MIN_9_MS                   (TIME_9_MS - DEV_9_MS)
105 #define    MAX_9_MS                   (TIME_9_MS + DEV_9_MS)
106
107 #define    TIME_42_MS                 (TIME_560_US * 75)
108 #define    DEV_42_MS                  (TIME_42_MS / 10)
109 #define    MIN_42_MS                  (TIME_42_MS - DEV_42_MS)
110 #define    MAX_42_MS                  (TIME_42_MS + DEV_42_MS)
```

Vector names have been redefined for the ability in the inner city codifying where. In the interruptible from the assembled start up, while you can see that I want the argument handler to interrupt, Vector corresponds to the external interrupt, configuring it for the infrared receiver data pin. And in the same way the timer three argu handler interrupt vector corresponds to the selected timer three. The NSC external ArcView Handler function is triggered when an infrared receiver output changes its logical level during the ongoing remote control command transmission. However, then, is it time to argue her functional behavior is different due to the system address and command decoding or repeat code receiving the firmware resets the time resculpting register to avoid the timers interrupt triggering. The time interrupt handler's purpose is to return the NSA decoder variables to the initial state. Assistant timeout occurs when the remote control does not send any pulses for more than 120 milliseconds. And the system timeout triggers the timer to interrupt, which calls the timer, or if you cannot function in such a situation, happens once after the release of a remote control button.

CLOCK CONFIGURATION FUNCTIONS

Now let's look at the RCC unit initialization sequence. In this team, 32 microcontrollers are crucial to follow the correct initialization sequence to obtain the expected results. For instance, each of the peripheral units involved in the system operation must have its clock enabled. Otherwise, the peripheral configuration registers cannot be retained by the initialization values. A function system called config initializes the system block by default, the system derives its Gloc from the internal 16 Mighell's frequency Althea's to later. Our task is to configure the 64 mental health system lock frequency. The arm cortex, CPU and internal flash memory work and different frequencies, the flash memory interface, latency and voltage scaling need to be adjusted accordingly.

```c
25 /* General System Init Function
26  *
27  */
28 void NEC_Decoder_Init(void)
29 {
30    LL_APB2_GRP1_EnableClock(LL_APB2_GRP1_PERIPH_SYSCFG);
31    LL_APB1_GRP1_EnableClock(LL_APB1_GRP1_PERIPH_PWR);
32    NVIC_SetPriorityGrouping(NVIC_PRIORITYGROUP_4);
33
34    SystemClock_Config();
35
36    GPIO_Init();
37
38    NEC_Timer_Init();
39 }
40
41
42 /**
43  * @brief System Clock Configuration
44  * @retval None
45  */
46 void SystemClock_Config(void)
47 {
48    LL_FLASH_SetLatency(LL_FLASH_LATENCY_2);
49
50    if(LL_FLASH_GetLatency() != LL_FLASH_LATENCY_2) {
51    Error_Handler();
52    }
53
54    LL_PWR_SetRegulVoltageScaling(LL_PWR_REGU_VOLTAGE_SCALE1);
55    LL_RCC_HSE_Enable();
56
57    // Wait till HSE is ready
58    while(LL_RCC_HSE_IsReady() != 1) {};
59
60    LL_RCC_PLL_ConfigDomain_SYS(LL_RCC_PLLSOURCE_HSE, LL_RCC_PLLM_DIV_4, 64, LL_RCC_PLLP_DIV_2);
61    LL_RCC_PLL_Enable();
62
63    // Wait till PLL is ready
64    while(LL_RCC_PLL_IsReady() != 1) {};
65
66    LL_RCC_SetAHBPrescaler(LL_RCC_SYSCLK_DIV_1);
67    LL_RCC_SetAPB1Prescaler(LL_RCC_APB1_DIV_2);
68    LL_RCC_SetAPB2Prescaler(LL_RCC_APB2_DIV_1);
69    LL_RCC_SetSysClkSource(LL_RCC_SYS_CLKSOURCE_PLL);
70
71    // Wait till System clock is ready
72    while(LL_RCC_GetSysClkSource() != LL_RCC_SYS_CLKSOURCE_STATUS_PLL) {};
73
74    LL_Init1msTick(64000000);
75    LL_SetSystemCoreClock(64000000);
76 }
77
78
79 /**
80  * GPIO Initialization Function
81  */
82 static void GPIO_Init(void)
```

Considering a power supply value and the selected CPU clock frequency, I will use the values provided by SDM to Cuba. Max. However, what is important for us is that the first step is the external aid megahertz frequency quartz crystal is enabled by this function alert to enable function.

The PLL input takes the external quartz crystal frequency as an input clock. When the external quartz crystal has stabilized and ready to use the PLL input, frequency, division and multiplication coefficients are selected according to the device clock three parameters from the SDM 30 to Cuba next to. After the PLL is enabled and stabilized, it can be used yet because its output frequency cannot exceed the maximum frequencies supported by a peripheral unit. The RCC initialization introduction mentioned that the SDM 32 internal peripherals support either 84 or 42 megahertz maximum clock frequency. For this reason, a preschooler divides by two the APB, one Busque lock frequency. Now, the 64 million health PLL clock can be selected as a primary system, Luxor's and the system peripherals can use it. This concludes the RCC unit initialization sequence description, but how to ensure that we have selected the right PLL frequency, which exactly corresponds to 64 megahertz. The simplest way of doing this is to use the timer scintillate handler.

GPIO AND EXTERNAL INTERRUPT TESTING

I know the board initialization requires more attention. The first step is enabling the clocks for all the iReports. The output beans from zero to four, six to seven and 12 to 15 are written with zeros to give the LCD switched over after the G.P.A. initialization. The same applies to the poor beeping five. This is done by writing the particular values into the port and port be beat, said reset registers. For the ladies, the G.P.A. is output, Push-Pull. The GPA, your Portmore, register enables the selected pince to work as output's, whereas the GPA, your output type register selects the Push-Pull GPA, your operating mode. The difference is that Paudie used the initialization structure, but the board uses direct writing to the board registers. It's possible to make this configuration without using the structures by direct writing into the registers. The outputs do not use the pull up and pull down resistors. The output speed register defines the GPA uSwitch in speed, and this register has its default value. The system configuration controller is used to manage the external interrupt line to be connected to the GPI. Since we use the I want interrupt vector in the MCU, the system configuration I see on one register is written with a value of zero zero one zero to I three to zero because it enables a precise one for the exterior. One interrupt. The edge detector configuration is performed by writing a logical one into the T one bit in both rising and falling trigger selection registers.

```
623  *           @arg @ref LL_SYSCFG_I2C_FASTMODEPLUS_SCL
624  *           @arg @ref LL_SYSCFG_I2C_FASTMODEPLUS_SDA
625  *           (*) value not defined in all devices
626  * @retval None
627  */
628  __STATIC_INLINE void LL_SYSCFG_DisableFastModePlus(uint32_t ConfigFastModePlus)
629  {
630    CLEAR_BIT(SYSCFG->CFGR, ConfigFastModePlus);
631  }
632  #endif /* SYSCFG_CFGR_FMPI2C1_SCL */
633
634  /**
635   * @brief  Configure source input for the EXTI external interrupt.
636   * @rmtoll SYSCFG_EXTICR1 EXTIx        LL_SYSCFG_SetEXTISource\n
637   *         SYSCFG_EXTICR2 EXTIx        LL_SYSCFG_SetEXTISource\n
638   *         SYSCFG_EXTICR3 EXTIx        LL_SYSCFG_SetEXTISource\n
639   *         SYSCFG_EXTICR4 EXTIx        LL_SYSCFG_SetEXTISource
640   * @param  Port This parameter can be one of the following values:
641   *           @arg @ref LL_SYSCFG_EXTI_PORTA
642   *           @arg @ref LL_SYSCFG_EXTI_PORTB
643   *           @arg @ref LL_SYSCFG_EXTI_PORTC
644   *           @arg @ref LL_SYSCFG_EXTI_PORTD
645   *           @arg @ref LL_SYSCFG_EXTI_PORTE
646   *           @arg @ref LL_SYSCFG_EXTI_PORTF (*)
647   *           @arg @ref LL_SYSCFG_EXTI_PORTG (*)
648   *           @arg @ref LL_SYSCFG_EXTI_PORTH
649   *
650   *           (*) value not defined in all devices
651   * @param  Line This parameter can be one of the following values:
652   *           @arg @ref LL_SYSCFG_EXTI_LINE0
653   *           @arg @ref LL_SYSCFG_EXTI_LINE1
654   *           @arg @ref LL_SYSCFG_EXTI_LINE2
655   *           @arg @ref LL_SYSCFG_EXTI_LINE3
656   *           @arg @ref LL_SYSCFG_EXTI_LINE4
657   *           @arg @ref LL_SYSCFG_EXTI_LINE5
658   *           @arg @ref LL_SYSCFG_EXTI_LINE6
659   *           @arg @ref LL_SYSCFG_EXTI_LINE7
660   *           @arg @ref LL_SYSCFG_EXTI_LINE8
661   *           @arg @ref LL_SYSCFG_EXTI_LINE9
662   *           @arg @ref LL_SYSCFG_EXTI_LINE10
663   *           @arg @ref LL_SYSCFG_EXTI_LINE11
664   *           @arg @ref LL_SYSCFG_EXTI_LINE12
665   *           @arg @ref LL_SYSCFG_EXTI_LINE13
666   *           @arg @ref LL_SYSCFG_EXTI_LINE14
667   *           @arg @ref LL_SYSCFG_EXTI_LINE15
668   * @retval None
669   */
670  __STATIC_INLINE void LL_SYSCFG_SetEXTISource(uint32_t Port, uint32_t Line)
671  {
672    MODIFY_REG(SYSCFG->EXTICR[Line & 0xFF], (Line >> 16), Port << POSITION_VAL((Line >> 16)));
673  }
674
675  /**
676   * @brief  Get the configured defined for specific EXTI Line
677   * @rmtoll SYSCFG_EXTICR1 EXTIx        LL_SYSCFG_GetEXTISource\n
678   *         SYSCFG_EXTICR2 EXTIx        LL_SYSCFG_GetEXTISource\n
679   *         SYSCFG_EXTICR3 EXTIx        LL_SYSCFG_GetEXTISource\n
680   *         SYSCFG_EXTICR4 EXTIx        LL_SYSCFG_GetEXTISource
```

The next step is to configure the PC one pin as an input with a pull up resistor, although the Infra-Red receiver contains a resistor connected to its open output. It's good to enable them to pull up resistor as well. To do this, the function LG your setting pull right away 01 into the Pupi the are one one two zero bit field in the port. Pull up. Pull down the resistor. Right in zeroth into the moat are one one two zero Busfield, or the corresponding port output register for Pawsey, configures the P.S. one pin as an input. Now, the GPA use an external internal configuration procedure is completed, now the NYC unit needs to be configured to sensor the external interrupt and pass it to the cortex. Sibiu to code lines are required once at the interoperability in the system and another one registers the interrupt vector in the visi. The external interrupt handler function is called NSC, external HQ handler, remember that they interrupt handlers never take or turn any parameters. Now it's time to test our configuration. A G.P.A. macro makes the code more readable, it simply redefines the peripheral library functions. Let us create a simple loop in the main function and write some values to the port pins to make them blink. And then let's flush them out to you as you see, the Elida output pins work as expected. Now, the external interrupt Trigorin needs to be tested, Lentulov handler requires two code lines to clear the external interrupt flex in both NBFC and I controllers. It allows avoiding the continuous interrupt handler function calling after the interrupt has occurred.

TIMER INITIALIZATION AND INTERRUPT TESTING

The timer three initialization is more detailed. At the beginning of the initial timer init function, the timer three state is returned to the reset state. Enabling the time or three ended in the RCC, EPB, one peripheral clock, and they have been registered, activates the timer peripheral clock. This language preprocessor calculates a time of scalar value for 10 microsecond resolution before the code compilation.

```c
63 #define          NEC_External_IRQ_Handler      EXTI1_IRQHandler
64 #define          NEC_EXTI_IRQn                 EXTI1_IRQn
65
66 // NEC Decoder Constants
67 #define          SYSTEM                        0
68 #define          FAULT                         0xFF
69 #define          MAX_BITS                      32
70 #define          START_OF_INV_SYS              9
71 #define          START_OF_COM                  17
72 #define          START_OF_INV_COM              25
73 #define          DECODE_IS_OK                  0x55
74
75 #define          INPUT_TIM_FREQUENCY           64000000 // 64 MHz Timer Clock
76 #define          FREQ_10_US                    100000
77 #define          TIME_SLOT_US                  10
78 #define          PULSE_LENGTH_US               560
79
80 #define          PRESCALER_10_US               (INPUT_TIM_FREQUENCY / FREQ_10_US)
81 #define          TIME_560_US                   (PULSE_LENGTH_US / TIME_SLOT_US)
82 #define          DEV_560_US                    TIME_560_US / 4
83 #define          MIN_560_US                    (TIME_560_US - DEV_560_US)
84 #define          MAX_560_US                    (TIME_560_US + DEV_560_US)
85
86 #define          TIME_1_125_MS                 (TIME_560_US * 2)
87 #define          DEV_1_125_MS                  (TIME_1_125_MS / 8)
88 #define          MIN_1_125_MS                  (TIME_1_125_MS - DEV_1_125_MS)
89 #define          MAX_1_125_MS                  (TIME_1_125_MS + DEV_1_125_MS)
90
91 #define          TIME_2_25_MS                  225
92 #define          DEV_2_25_MS                   (TIME_2_25_MS / 8)
93 #define          MIN_2_25_MS                   (TIME_2_25_MS - DEV_2_25_MS)
94 #define          MAX_2_25_MS                   (TIME_2_25_MS + DEV_2_25_MS)
95
96 #define          TIME_4_5_MS                   (TIME_2_25_MS * 2)
97 #define          DEV_4_5_MS                    (TIME_4_5_MS / 8)
98 #define          MIN_4_5_MS                    (TIME_4_5_MS - DEV_4_5_MS)
99 #define          MAX_4_5_MS                    (TIME_4_5_MS + DEV_4_5_MS)
100
101 #define         TIME_9_MS                     (TIME_4_5_MS * 2)
102 #define         DEV_9_MS                      (TIME_9_MS / 8)
103 #define         MIN_9_MS                      (TIME_9_MS - DEV_9_MS)
104 #define         MAX_9_MS                      (TIME_9_MS + DEV_9_MS)
105
106 #define         TIME_42_MS                    (TIME_560_US * 75)
107 #define         DEV_42_MS                     (TIME_42_MS / 10)
108 #define         MIN_42_MS                     (TIME_42_MS - DEV_42_MS)
109 #define         MAX_42_MS                     (TIME_42_MS + DEV_42_MS)
110
111 #define         TIME_98_MS                    (TIME_560_US * 175)
112 #define         DEV_98_MS                     (TIME_98_MS / 10)
113 #define         MIN_98_MS                     (TIME_98_MS - DEV_98_MS)
114 #define         MAX_98_MS                     (TIME_98_MS + DEV_98_MS)
115
116 #define         TIME_120_MS                   (TIME_560_US * 214)
117
118 #endif /* __NEC_IR_H */
```

The 60 former first timers put frequency is divided by the 10 microseconds corresponding frequency equal to 100 kilohertz. By this means, the rescaling value of 640 is calculated and it will be written into the 16 bit time three a little register. It allows the timer to be incremented by one every 10 microseconds. The following parameter indicates that Timer three will be an up counter for this, they are a bit in the timer control. Register one is return zero. The time to reload the register contains the maximum possible accounting value, and it will be F F, F F in hexadecimal form. Close division structure field defines a ratio between the time of the clock and the digital field resembling a clock. In our case, their frequencies match each other and zeros are written into the second one to zero bit field in the timer control register one.

```
118 /**
119  * Timer 3 Initialization Function
120  */
121 static void NEC_Timer_Init(void)
122 {
123     LL_TIM_InitTypeDef TIM_InitStruct = {0};
124
125     // Reset the timer peripheral unit.
126     LL_TIM_DeInit(NEC_Timer);
127
128     // Peripheral clock enable
129     LL_APB1_GRP1_EnableClock(RCC_APB_Periph_NEC_Timer);
130
131     TIM_InitStruct.Prescaler = PRESCALER_10_US;
132     TIM_InitStruct.CounterMode = LL_TIM_COUNTERMODE_UP; // Up counter
133     TIM_InitStruct.Autoreload = 0xFFFF; // The maximum possible counter's value
134     TIM_InitStruct.ClockDivision = LL_TIM_CLOCKDIVISION_DIV1;
135     LL_TIM_Init(TIM3, &TIM_InitStruct);
136
137     LL_TIM_DisableARRPreload(NEC_Timer);
138
139     LL_TIM_SetClockSource(NEC_Timer, LL_TIM_CLOCKSOURCE_INTERNAL);
140     LL_TIM_DisableMasterSlaveMode(NEC_Timer);
141
142     // Set a compare value for channel 1
143     LL_TIM_OC_SetCompareCH1(NEC_Timer, TIME_120_MS); // 120 ms timeout
144
145     // Enable Compare interrupt for timer 3
146     LL_TIM_EnableIT_CC1(NEC_Timer);
147
148     // TIM3_IRQn interrupt configuration
149     NVIC_SetPriority(NEC_Timer_IRQn, NVIC_EncodePriority(NVIC_GetPriorityGrouping(),7, 0));
150     NVIC_EnableIRQ(NEC_Timer_IRQn);
151 }
152
153
154 /* This function returns the NEC
155  * decoder to its initial state
156  */
157 void NEC_Timer_IRQ_Handler(void)
158 {
159 }
160
161
162 /* This function handles
163  * the IR receiver's output
164  */
165 void NEC_External_IRQ_Handler(void)
166 {
167 }
```

And not to reload, reload, timers function is not used and this function disables it. Writing Zeros to the Easy and Smith two to zero beats in the time or slave mode, Control Register selects the internal clock as an input clock for timer three. The following function disables the MSM bit in the same timeously remote control register, which means the timer three is not synchronized. These are the timers. They compare value as an essential parameter for the inner decoder. Timer three has four compelling channels. The first compelling channel will be used in a city called. When a compelling value matches the timeless countless value, the output compare event triggers the timer three interrupt.

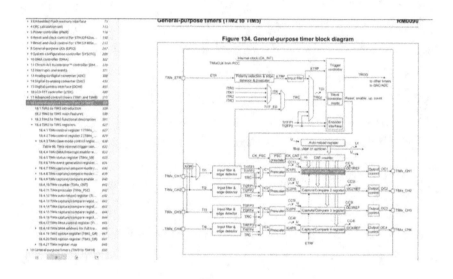

For one hundred twenty milliseconds, the preprocessor calculates a timeless, compelling value as a five hundred sixty microsecond time slot multiplied by two hundred fourteen equal to eleven thousand nine hundred eighty four. Eleven thousand nine hundred eighty four multiplied by a 10 second time slot, gives approximately almost 120 millisecond timeout period for the initial recorded. The obtained value eleven thousand nine hundred eighty four is written into the time of three.

Capture compare register one. The last code line is an interrupt activation function for timer three, Channel one. It enables this issue one I beat in the time or three, interrupt and they register and makes the campaign interrupt visible for the NDIC. Now, the NBA needs to be initialized to globally enable this, interrupting the system, the same analogy applies as it has been with the external interrupt initialization. The timer complaint dropped is assigned to the priority in the system and registered by two code lines at the end of the NSC timer init function. The anytime Eric Handler function is a timer handler. The whole time or initialization procedure for the NSA, the Cordy's completed. For interrupt triggering testing purposes, the compare value will be changed to one temporarily. Such a change of the compare value will demonstrate the timeless standard for a second measurement accuracy. As we did with interrupt flags of the external interrupt, the timer interrupts, we clear the necessary interrupt flex. The orange alert macro will be used again to change the state. Right, analogical one into the sea and bit in the timer three control register activates the county remote in time or three. In the inner city code, the algorithm, the external interrupter will trigger this timer.

The low level timer had down to function, resets the timer, and three counting registers value. If we compile and run the binary into the MCU, the orange lady will be told every time the timer compare interrupt handler is called. If we record any time and diagram biologic analyzer and then check this diagram, we can confirm that the time has come to interrupt is triggered exactly every 10 seconds. Let us change the compelling value to its default value. Now we see that the lady blinks several times per second. A slight time mismatch is not critical for the time generation. Now we have initialized them to you and can start to implement them and see the quadrilogy. Thanks for watching and thanks for active participation.

```
 95 #define        Set_Green                   LL_GPIO_SetOutputPin(Green_Port, Green_Pin);
 96 #define        Set_Orange                  LL_GPIO_SetOutputPin(Orange_Port, Orange_Pin);
 97 #define        Set_Red                     LL_GPIO_SetOutputPin(Red_Port, Red_Pin);
 98 #define        Set_Blue                    LL_GPIO_SetOutputPin(Blue_Port, Blue_Pin);
 99 #define        Set_LED5                    LL_GPIO_SetOutputPin(LED5_Port, LED5_Pin);
100 #define        Set_LED6                    LL_GPIO_SetOutputPin(LED6_Port, LED6_Pin);
101
102 #define        Reset_Green                 LL_GPIO_ResetOutputPin(Green_Port, Green_Pin);
103 #define        Reset_Orange                LL_GPIO_ResetOutputPin(Orange_Port, Orange_Pin)
104 #define        Reset_Red                   LL_GPIO_ResetOutputPin(Red_Port, Red_Pin);
105 #define        Reset_Blue                  LL_GPIO_ResetOutputPin(Blue_Port, Blue_Pin);
106 #define        Reset_LED5                  LL_GPIO_ResetOutputPin(LED5_Port, LED5_Pin);
107 #define        Reset_LED6                  LL_GPIO_ResetOutputPin(LED6_Port, LED6_Pin);
108
109 #define        Toggle_Green                LL_GPIO_TogglePin(Green_Port, Green_Pin);
110 #define        Toggle_Orange               LL_GPIO_TogglePin(Orange_Port, Orange_Pin);
111 #define        Toggle_Red                  LL_GPIO_TogglePin(Red_Port, Red_Pin);
112 #define        Toggle_Blue                 LL_GPIO_TogglePin(Blue_Port, Blue_Pin);
113 #define        Toggle_LED5                 LL_GPIO_TogglePin(LED5_Port, LED5_Pin);
114 #define        Toggle_LED6                 LL_GPIO_TogglePin(LED6_Port, LED6_Pin);
115
116 // LEDs defines
117 //
118 #define        Green_Port                  GPIOD
119 #define        Green_Pin                   LL_GPIO_PIN_12
120
121 #define        Orange_Port                 GPIOD
122 #define        Orange_Pin                  LL_GPIO_PIN_13
123
124 #define        Red_Port                    GPIOD
125 #define        Red_Pin                     LL_GPIO_PIN_14
126
127 #define        Blue_Port                   GPIOD
128 #define        Blue_Pin                    LL_GPIO_PIN_15
129
130 #define        LED5_Port                   GPIOD
131 #define        LED5_Pin                    LL_GPIO_PIN_0
132
133 #define        LED6_Port                   GPIOD
134 #define        LED6_Pin                    LL_GPIO_PIN_1
135
136
137 // Buttons codes
138 //
139 #define        Ch_P            71
140 #define        Channel         70
141 #define        Ch_M            69
142 #define        PREV            68
143 #define        NEXT            64
144 #define        PLAY            67
145 #define        VOL_PLUS        7
146 #define        VOL_MINUS       21
147 #define        EQ              9
148 #define        ZERO            22
149 #define        PLUS_100        25
150 #define        PLUS_200        13
151 #define        ONE            
```

The orange bellied toggling macro in words, the latest state when the external Interop handler function is called. Now the binary into the MCU. A logic analyzer can help to compare the infrared receiver's output pin and the latest timing diagrams, Channel three shows the infrared receiver output state, whereas Channel two is connected to the. If we press any button on the remote control, we can see that the orange alert is blinking. The diagram comparison confirms that each state change of the orange already corresponds to its. I want an external interrupt. The timing diagram recorded from the lady shows the remote control bid values without inversion. We see that both diamond diagrams I inverted, but they correspond entirely to each other.

NEC PROTOCOL MAIN DECODING LOGIC

Will explain the initiative called Core Logic Implementation, providing that the NSA decoder is completely interrupted, driven the Internet can contain the decoding algorithm logic. Let us consider the algorithm of the external Interop handler first. As mentioned in the previous course lectures, the external interrupt handler is called when the infrared receiver output data pin levels changes. Both rising and falling ages triggered the external interrupt whenever this interrupt, this triggered the fireworks, the received pulse length, knowing the measured pulse length and the current decoder state, the system can understand which kind of data is currently received from the remote control. The agency Pulse is received first and its length is measured, followed by a 4.5 millisecond pulse. Then the system address and the inventor's system address are decoded, the same applies to the command and inverted command decoding. When both system and command are received, the NSC decoder continuously checks the repeat codes, the reception. Whenever the repeat code is received, the repeat code counter is incremented. Now, what happens if a button on the remote control is released? They still interrupt and there will not be called on this occasion anymore, and the time will not be restarted for a new measurement cycle.

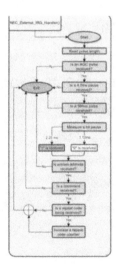 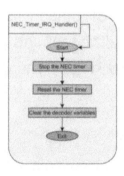

If there are no pulses received for 120 milliseconds, then the timer of three campaign teret is called and returns the NSC decoder to the initial state. But let us analyze the external interrupt handler quote more deeply. When the external interrupt is called, the interrupt lights are cleared in both timer and the visi. Then the timer counters value is read to a variable, and this variable value defines the length between two nabor edges in the transmission. When the remote control transmits a thirty 38 kilohertz frequency, the receiver's output is zero. Litchfield's detected edge will not provide the measurement result because the timer is stopped at this stage. And the timer is started by name when they see and beat in the time or three control register one. The next day, the state agency end is assigned to this system, and the logic expects the next rising age from the receiver, when the age arrives, the time has come to register. Value is read. The measure that value is nine milliseconds, the timer is restarted to measure the four and half millisecond pause and the decoding stage is changed to the short pause.

```
313  */
314  void NEC_External_IRQ_Handler (void)
315  {
316      uint16_t len = 0;
317
318      NVIC_ClearPendingIRQ(NEC_EXTI_IRQn);
319      LL_EXTI_ClearFlag_0_31(IR_RECEIVER_LINE);
320
321      len = read_nec_timer();                          // Get the pulse len
322
323      switch (decoding_state)
324      {
325      case AGC_START:
326          start_nec_timer();                           // Start 9 ms pulse measurement
327          decoding_state = AGC_END;                    // Begin decoding
328          return;
329
330      case AGC_END:
331          reset_nec_timer();                           // Reset timer
332          if ((len > MIN_9_MS) && (len < MAX_9_MS))    // ... 9 ms AGC
333          {
334              decoding_state = SHORT_PAUSE;            // then begin a 4.5 ms..
335              return;                                  // ..pulse measurement
336          }
337          break;
338
339      case SHORT_PAUSE:
340          reset_nec_timer();                           // Reset timer
341          if ((len > MIN_4_5_MS) && (len < MAX_4_5_MS))
342          {
343              decoding_state = NEC_ADDR_COMM;          // Begin system adress decode
344              return;
345          }
346          break;
347
348      case NEC_ADDR_COMM:
349          if ((len > MIN_560_US) && (len < MAX_560_US) &&
350              (bitn == MAX_BITS) &&
351              ((system & inv_system) == 0) &&
352              ((command & inv_command) == 0))
353          {
354              decoding_state = LONG_PAUSE_1;           // Begin a long pause measurement
355              reset_nec_timer();                       // Reset timer
356              bitn = DECODE_IS_OK;
357              LED_Control();
358              return;
359          }
360          else
361          {
362              decoding_state = NEC_BITS_DEC;
363              return;
364          }
365          break;
366
367      case NEC_BITS_DEC:                               // Bits receiving
368          reset_nec_timer();                           // Reset timer
369          decoding_state = NEC_ADDR_COMM;
370          bitn++;
```

When the front edge of the first received systematized bit
is detected, the pauses length is measured before the bit
length measurement occurs, the following state and the
address command is assigned to the decoder state
machine. Thus, each high or low logical level length is

known when a new measurement has started at the following edge. After the four and half millisecond pulse, the first bit of the system address is received and the firmware will check the pulse length. After that in the NSC meets the coding section of the decoder, the pauses are measured. At two point twenty five millisecond pause period corresponds to the logical one received, whereas at one point twelve millisecond pause interval is a logical zero. When all the address and command bits are received, the decoder enters a long post, one state restarts the timer and expects to receive the repeat called a function, and the control is called to change the elitist status. Before the first repeat call, this received approximately 14 millisecond Berserkers. And then logically and then millisecond agency pulse at two point twenty five millisecond space and five hundred sixty microsecond burst, followed by a 40 millisecond pause. Then the decoding state is changed to the long post to end up at approximately 98 milliseconds, the repeat code is received again. A repeat called county increases its value by one each time when the repeat code is received, the repeat code county can be helpful when measuring how long the remote control button has been held. At this stage, nothing else happens in the system until the button on the remote control is released. When there is no pulse from the remote control for more than 120 milliseconds, the timer's compare value matches the time counter registered value and the timer complaint drop is triggered. First, the timelessly drop handler closed, interruptive legs stopped, Taimur, three, cleared its content register and prepared the NSC decoder for the next command reception. Then its indicative variables are returned to their initial state, a function and the control is called to change the elitist status, and at this point, the timer interrupts, Handler doesn't do more. The following timer start will be initiated when the button on the remote control will be pressed again in the following lecture will analyze a few auxiliary functions used over an AC protocol decoded.

AUXILIARY NEC DECODER FUNCTIONS

These functions are used for improving the country's ability and for changing the status. The first two functions which require attention and are used by the NSC decoder, as known, are received and one is received. These functions are received with value to the system in the system, command and inverted command variables. Analogical zero or a logical one is told to be the most inefficient with seven biological shifts to the right. A bit West End operator is used to three logical zero. Maybe twice or operator is used to store a logical one.

```
1299    * @brief  Get the counter value.
1300    * @note Macro IS_TIM_32B_COUNTER_INSTANCE(TIMx) can be used to check
1301    *       whether or not a timer instance supports a 32 bits counter.
1302    * @rmtoll CNT          CNT           LL_TIM_GetCounter
1303    * @param  TIMx Timer instance
1304    * @retval Counter value (between Min_Data=0 and Max_Data=0xFFFF or 0xFFFFFFFF)
1305    */
1306   __STATIC_INLINE uint32_t LL_TIM_GetCounter(TIM_TypeDef *TIMx)
1307   {
1308     return (uint32_t)(READ_REG(TIMx->CNT));
1309   }
1310
1311   /**
1312    * @brief  Get the current direction of the counter
1313    * @rmtoll CR1          DIR           LL_TIM_GetDirection
1314    * @param  TIMx Timer instance
1315    * @retval Returned value can be one of the following values:
1316    *         @arg @ref LL_TIM_COUNTERDIRECTION_UP
1317    *         @arg @ref LL_TIM_COUNTERDIRECTION_DOWN
1318    */
1319   __STATIC_INLINE uint32_t LL_TIM_GetDirection(TIM_TypeDef *TIMx)
1320   {
1321     return (uint32_t)(READ_BIT(TIMx->CR1, TIM_CR1_DIR));
1322   }
1323
1324   /**
1325    * @brief  Set the prescaler value.
1326    * @note The counter clock frequency CK_CNT is equal to fCK_PSC / (PSC[15:0] + 1).
1327    * @note The prescaler can be changed on the fly as this control register is buffered. The new
1328    *       prescaler ratio is taken into account at the next update event.
1329    * @note Helper macro @ref __LL_TIM_CALC_PSC can be used to calculate the Prescaler parameter
1330    * @rmtoll PSC          PSC           LL_TIM_SetPrescaler
1331    * @param  TIMx Timer instance
1332    * @param  Prescaler between Min_Data=0 and Max_Data=65535
1333    * @retval None
1334    */
1335   __STATIC_INLINE void LL_TIM_SetPrescaler(TIM_TypeDef *TIMx, uint32_t Prescaler)
1336   {
1337     WRITE_REG(TIMx->PSC, Prescaler);
1338   }
1339
1340   /**
1341    * @brief  Get the prescaler value.
1342    * @rmtoll PSC          PSC           LL_TIM_GetPrescaler
1343    * @param  TIMx Timer instance
1344    * @retval Prescaler value between Min_Data=0 and Max_Data=65535
1345    */
1346   __STATIC_INLINE uint32_t LL_TIM_GetPrescaler(TIM_TypeDef *TIMx)
1347   {
1348     return (uint32_t)(READ_REG(TIMx->PSC));
1349   }
1350
1351   /**
1352    * @brief  Set the auto-reload value.
1353    * @note The counter is blocked while the auto-reload value is null.
1354    * @note Macro IS_TIM_32B_COUNTER_INSTANCE(TIMx) can be used to check
1355    *       whether or not a timer instance supports a 32 bits counter.
1356    * @note Helper macro @ref __LL_TIM_CALC_ARR can be used to calculate the AutoReload parameter
```

The function started as a timer and stopped an AC timer to represent a simple obstruction interface to the low level peripheral drivers. These functions enable or disable the sea and beat in the time or three control register one, which starts or stops the counting. A function is the timer returns, the timer counting the registered value. A function that we set in is a timer reset of the timer counting the register. aFunction gets an exhibit and state checks if a command has been decoded the functions and gets any system state and gets any command state provided the coded system address and the command. The functionality control rights reserved command to port in Port B and toggles the four Allardice on the Discovery Board if a corresponding button on the remote control is pressed at this point, we have recovered the auxiliary functions.

NEC DECODER TESTING

Now we are ready to test our new city called on this day after the two for Discovery more. If we open a file in the civil rights section, we can tell the compiler to what extent the code should be optimized. A few compiler optimization levels are available for us, minus OO optimizations for compilation time, minus one optimization for good size and execution time minus two and minus all three. Optimization more for code size and execution time minus OS optimization for code size or each compiler optimization option.

Optimization flag	.text section size	.data section size	nec_decoder.bin size
-O0	7092	12	7104
-O1	3764	12	3776
-O2	3584	12	3596
-O3	3592	12	3604
-Os	3476	12	3488

We will get a different code size and see you executable. Binary file size consists of a sum of the text and data sections I have compiled and see the code with the different optimization options as we see different compiler optimization levels provide a different file size and not always the higher optimization level is better. Let's compile when you see the code without optimization. By type in last month's file filename, we can check that the binary file size is exactly seven thousand one hundred four bytes, confirming that everything is correct. The text section is seven thousand ninety two bytes while the data section is twelve bytes. However, this optimization provides the smallest output binary file size.

```
researcher@regulus-RnD:~/NEC_Decoder/nec_decoder$
researcher@regulus-RnD:~/NEC_Decoder/nec_decoder$
researcher@regulus-RnD:~/NEC_Decoder/nec_decoder$ make
mkdir build
arm-none-eabi-gcc -c -mcpu=cortex-m4 -mthumb -mfpu=fpv4-sp-d16 -mfloat-abi=hard -DUSE_FULL_LL_DRIVER
LUE=12288000 -DHSI_VALUE=16000000 -DLSI_VALUE=32000 -DVDD_VALUE=3300 -DPREFETCH_ENABLE=1 -DINSTRUCTI
Device/ST/STM32F4xx/Include -IDrivers/CMSIS/Include -IDrivers/CMSIS/Include -Og -Wall -fdata-section
build/main.o
arm-none-eabi-gcc -c -mcpu=cortex-m4 -mthumb -mfpu=fpv4-sp-d16 -mfloat-abi=hard -DUSE_FULL_LL_DRIVER
LUE=12288000 -DHSI_VALUE=16000000 -DLSI_VALUE=32000 -DVDD_VALUE=3300 -DPREFETCH_ENABLE=1 -DINSTRUCTI
Device/ST/STM32F4xx/Include -IDrivers/CMSIS/Include -IDrivers/CMSIS/Include -Og -Wall -fdata-section
R.c -o build/NEC_IR.o
arm-none-eabi-gcc -c -mcpu=cortex-m4 -mthumb -mfpu=fpv4-sp-d16 -mfloat-abi=hard -DUSE_FULL_LL_DRIVER
LUE=12288000 -DHSI_VALUE=16000000 -DLSI_VALUE=32000 -DVDD_VALUE=3300 -DPREFETCH_ENABLE=1 -DINSTRUCTI
Device/ST/STM32F4xx/Include -IDrivers/CMSIS/Include -IDrivers/CMSIS/Include -Og -Wall -fdata-section
st Src/stm32f4xx_it.c -o build/stm32f4xx_it.o
arm-none-eabi-gcc -c -mcpu=cortex-m4 -mthumb -mfpu=fpv4-sp-d16 -mfloat-abi=hard -DUSE_FULL_LL_DRIVER
LUE=12288000 -DHSI_VALUE=16000000 -DLSI_VALUE=32000 -DVDD_VALUE=3300 -DPREFETCH_ENABLE=1 -DINSTRUCTI
Device/ST/STM32F4xx/Include -IDrivers/CMSIS/Include -IDrivers/CMSIS/Include -Og -Wall -fdata-section
_ll_gpio.lst Drivers/STM32F4xx_HAL_Driver/Src/stm32f4xx_ll_gpio.c -o build/stm32f4xx_ll_gpio.o
arm-none-eabi-gcc -c -mcpu=cortex-m4 -mthumb -mfpu=fpv4-sp-d16 -mfloat-abi=hard -DUSE_FULL_LL_DRIVER
LUE=12288000 -DHSI_VALUE=16000000 -DLSI_VALUE=32000 -DVDD_VALUE=3300 -DPREFETCH_ENABLE=1 -DINSTRUCTI
Device/ST/STM32F4xx/Include -IDrivers/CMSIS/Include -IDrivers/CMSIS/Include -Og -Wall -fdata-section
ll_tim.lst Drivers/STM32F4xx_HAL_Driver/Src/stm32f4xx_ll_tim.c -o build/stm32f4xx_ll_tim.o
arm-none-eabi-gcc -c -mcpu=cortex-m4 -mthumb -mfpu=fpv4-sp-d16 -mfloat-abi=hard -DUSE_FULL_LL_DRIVER
LUE=12288000 -DHSI_VALUE=16000000 -DLSI_VALUE=32000 -DVDD_VALUE=3300 -DPREFETCH_ENABLE=1 -DINSTRUCTI
Device/ST/STM32F4xx/Include -IDrivers/CMSIS/Include -IDrivers/CMSIS/Include -Og -Wall -fdata-section
ll_dma.lst Drivers/STM32F4xx_HAL_Driver/Src/stm32f4xx_ll_dma.c -o build/stm32f4xx_ll_dma.o
arm-none-eabi-gcc -c -mcpu=cortex-m4 -mthumb -mfpu=fpv4-sp-d16 -mfloat-abi=hard -DUSE_FULL_LL_DRIVER
LUE=12288000 -DHSI_VALUE=16000000 -DLSI_VALUE=32000 -DVDD_VALUE=3300 -DPREFETCH_ENABLE=1 -DINSTRUCTI
Device/ST/STM32F4xx/Include -IDrivers/CMSIS/Include -IDrivers/CMSIS/Include -Og -Wall -fdata-section
ll_rcc.lst Drivers/STM32F4xx_HAL_Driver/Src/stm32f4xx_ll_rcc.c -o build/stm32f4xx_ll_rcc.o
arm-none-eabi-gcc -c -mcpu=cortex-m4 -mthumb -mfpu=fpv4-sp-d16 -mfloat-abi=hard -DUSE_FULL_LL_DRIVER
LUE=12288000 -DHSI_VALUE=16000000 -DLSI_VALUE=32000 -DVDD_VALUE=3300 -DPREFETCH_ENABLE=1 -DINSTRUCTI
Device/ST/STM32F4xx/Include -IDrivers/CMSIS/Include -IDrivers/CMSIS/Include -Og -Wall -fdata-section
x_ll_utils.lst Drivers/STM32F4xx_HAL_Driver/Src/stm32f4xx_ll_utils.c -o build/stm32f4xx_ll_utils.o
arm-none-eabi-gcc -c -mcpu=cortex-m4 -mthumb -mfpu=fpv4-sp-d16 -mfloat-abi=hard -DUSE_FULL_LL_DRIVER
LUE=12288000 -DHSI_VALUE=16000000 -DLSI_VALUE=32000 -DVDD_VALUE=3300 -DPREFETCH_ENABLE=1 -DINSTRUCTI
Device/ST/STM32F4xx/Include -IDrivers/CMSIS/Include -IDrivers/CMSIS/Include -Og -Wall -fdata-section
_ll_exti.lst Drivers/STM32F4xx_HAL_Driver/Src/stm32f4xx_ll_exti.c -o build/stm32f4xx_ll_exti.o
arm-none-eabi-gcc -c -mcpu=cortex-m4 -mthumb -mfpu=fpv4-sp-d16 -mfloat-abi=hard -DUSE_FULL_LL_DRIVER
LUE=12288000 -DHSI_VALUE=16000000 -DLSI_VALUE=32000 -DVDD_VALUE=3300 -DPREFETCH_ENABLE=1 -DINSTRUCTI
Device/ST/STM32F4xx/Include -IDrivers/CMSIS/Include -IDrivers/CMSIS/Include -Og -Wall -fdata-section
32f4xx.lst Src/system_stm32f4xx.c -o build/system_stm32f4xx.o
arm-none-eabi-gcc -x assembler-with-cpp -c -mcpu=cortex-m4 -mthumb -mfpu=fpv4-sp-d16 -mfloat-abi=har
68 -DEXTERNAL_CLOCK_VALUE=12288000 -DHSI_VALUE=16000000 -DLSI_VALUE=32000 -DVDD_VALUE=3300 -DPREFETC
r/Inc -IDrivers/CMSIS/Device/ST/STM32F4xx/Include -IDrivers/CMSIS/Include -IDrivers/CMSIS/Include -C
stm32f407xx.s -o build/startup_stm32f407xx.o
arm-none-eabi-gcc build/main.o build/NEC_IR.o build/stm32f4xx_it.o build/stm32f4xx_ll_gpio.o build/s
ll_exti.o build/system_stm32f4xx.o build/startup_stm32f407xx.o -mcpu=cortex-m4 -mthumb -mfpu=fpv4-sp
ap,--cref -Wl,--gc-sections -o build/nec_decoder.elf
arm-none-eabi-size build/nec_decoder.elf
   text    data     bss     dec     hex filename
   7092      12    1580    8684    21ec build/nec_decoder.elf
arm-none-eabi-objcopy -O ihex build/nec_decoder.elf build/nec_decoder.hex
arm-none-eabi-objcopy -O binary -S build/nec_decoder.elf build/nec_decoder.bin
researcher@regulus-RnD:~/NEC_Decoder/nec_decoder$ ls -l build/nec_decoder.bin
-rwxrwxr-x 1 researcher researcher 7104 mai  28 19:28 build/nec_decoder.bin
```

It is connected to the Discovery Board indicating they received command of the remote control and the ladies are switched off by the button on the remote control is released. Some of the buttons controlled Daily News on the discovery board. Thus, if I press the standby button, I can activate the other buttons, mute input and sound change. The orange, red and blue LCD, respectively. By changing the predefined button called constants in the main each file, it's possible to assign the different buttons to control the LCD.

WHAT IS AN RTOS

So let's start analyzing what an artist is and what it does. Artist stands for real time operating system and the very quick and dirty if you will definition of a real time operating system is that it does the right thing at the right time otherwise things go terribly horribly wrong. Examples of real time operating systems can be found in many places and in fact if you are looking at the screen at the moment which I think there is a quite high likelihood that you are doing well behind the scenes on your screen there should be a microcontroller and that the microcontroller is more than likely using a real Palm operating system for doing its thing. Well it could be other things in there as well and if you have a wireless mouse it will have an operating system. And if it has an operating system it will be a real time operating system as well. And of course there are different types of real time systems. So what you're looking at is a fighter jet on the screen. And the interesting thing about the fight there is that if something goes horribly horribly wrong with that fighter jet it is possible that it will fall out of the sky or it will do something silly like firing a missile where it shouldn't do a bad thing about this. He's quite well equipped. They normally fighter jets are quite well equipped with missiles. So real time operating systems effectively come in different flavors of real time ness if you will. If I could actually put it this way and what I mean by saying this is that there are different types of things that can go wrong when you're using a real time operating system. So if you have a real help rating system for a fighter jet you will have to architect your system in a different way rather than if you have a real time operating system for I don't know perhaps something like a washing machine or a mouse or your light ball but home and I do have one of those light bulbs actually at the moment lighting my roof. So there are quite a number of things that can go horribly horribly wrong if you have a fighter jet. However if your light bulb turns on or 10 this caller maybe 10 milliseconds later than normal then it's While if for example a fighter jet does something 10 milliseconds later than it should do and it might follow this guy and that's not fine as you might think. So yes you can use a real time operating system and there are many real time operating systems. It is in fact possible to create a real time operating system and make it operate in a non real time manner. That means that it will generally work, however the timing tolerances as to when the reaction time is complete with respect to an input can be fairly loose. So you say I push a button and it doesn't really matter if an action happens within 100 milliseconds or within 500 milliseconds while on different use cases you might say when I push this button in 25 microseconds I must have a reaction. Okay. And there are cases such as in the automotive industry for example or in the aerospace industry where this is the case. So autos provide a number of abstract constructs that help monitor execution of different tasks in a timely and predictable manner. It creates and manages different tasks that are also referred to as threads. So you might hear me talking about tasks or threads or processes and actually these three words will be used interchangeably throughout the course in autos defining certain abstract structures to manage access to also serially reusable resources such as parts of memory networks and so on. The theory here is that for example you might only have one network port or only one a U.S. report and then you have three different processes for different threads that want to communicate with this one port so that the operating system is going to actually manage access to this port making sure that only one process has access to it at the time. The problem is of course if you have multiple processes having access to the same UDP port at the same time then you might have data corruption or things might not work properly. So your operating system provides some structures to manage this access and throughout this course we'll look at those in a lot more detail. Real time operating systems will also prioritize different threads or tasks or processes so accurately there will be different priorities. You can imagine for example inside that car at your window suite has a different priority from your IBS commands. If it is operating on the same processor typically it wouldn't but if it did because of course it doesn't really matter if we 100 milliseconds later responds when we post that window switch. However if for some reason the B.S. takes 100 milliseconds more to respond to a certain type of input this might actually end up very very badly and people are going to feel very bad very soon. So an operating system also manages harmonious executions of all threads and serially reusable resources. That is to say that the operating system is acting as a master scheduler of everything that needs to happen and ensures that everything happens smoothly and that everything cooperates with itself provided that you have programmed it properly. In this course I will show you how to do exactly that. Okay so an operating system can be thought of as operating in two different domains simultaneously. One of those domains is monetizing the access to resources and another domain is monetizing access to the time off the main processor. Now if you have one core now there are multiple courses. There is a possibility to have multiple courses in a certain system on the tape SLC as we call them. So it is extremely important that you have an operating system which has the capability and has been programmed appropriately to monetize both data and processor time for each one of its threads or processes it is possible and indeed it is even common to Jews and our toes for non real time application such as for example a washing machine or a vending machine or I don't know what I have right in front of me as a Power Bank. So there is some type of artist in there even if it is going to be fairly fairly bare bones types of application that well it manages my part wrong. There is another thing in front of me which is a calculator or there should be some sort of art in there actually managing how this calculator works. It is possible that his art assists will be more or less complicated or some of those devices might even be bare bones but it is highly likely that they will have a real time operating system. The thing is a real term operating system adds some process or overhead because of course it needs to run all of its own processes and it is not going to be less efficient to run with an operating system than to run bare bones as in without an operating system.

RTOS

- Real-Time Operating System
- Provides a number of constructs that help manage execution of different tasks in a timely and predictable manner
- Creates and manages different tasks are also referred to as Threads (depending the language conventions that different RTOSs like to use)
- Defines structures to manage access to serially reusable resources such as parts of memory, networks etc.
- Issues priorities to threads/tasks
- Manages harmonious execution of all threads and serially re-usable resources
- Operates in 2 different domains simultaneously
  - Managing access to data/resources
  - Managing access to the time of the processor
- It is possible (and indeed even common) to use an RTOS for a non real-time application
- An RTOS doesn't make an application real-time & safety critical. You have to know how to use an RTOS to make a safety critical application perform in a time-defined manner

A Real Time Operating System does
- **The right thing**
- **At the right time**

Otherwise things go horribly horribly wrong

Smart Light Bulb
FOR HOME WIFI Control

However typically you will find that people want to have an operating system because actually we have very fast process force nowadays at very very low cost and the development cost of a product which does not use an operating system will be higher than to pay the costs of the extra cost for a little bit more powerful hardware and in the long run. It doesn't it doesn't work out economically. So you prefer to use an operating system even though you could do it bare bones because your development costs are lower. My first double were creating some sort of device that manages audio amplifiers and what we were actually doing is we're saying okay let's put a little bit of a more expensive pressure in here so that we can fit an operating system and it doesn't really matter that this process is going to cost a tiny bit more than if we did it without an operating system because actually the benefits of having very quick development and well manage the processes in a safe way outweighs the costs of paying for a little bit higher and more expensive hardware. An artist doesn't make an application real time and safety critical. You have to know how to use an artist to make safety critical applications perform in a time defined manner of course. If for example I were the clothes of a gardener then I'd have gone to some gardening that does not automatically make me a master gardener. Gardening is an art and it needs a lot of effort to master it. Just like creating proper real time operating systems and creating real time operating system applications that work in a time defined manner is an art. It takes a lot of time to master it.

THE CMSIS RTOS API

In this section we will explore what the CMC is. Are those API what it does and how we're going to use it throughout this course. So this course explains real time operating systems and it uses as an example the arty x5 operating system RDX is the name of the operating system five's version and the CMC is Arthur's version to API and then we're using those in the context of the SDM 32 F for family of our cortex and for microcontrollers now it is worth saying here of course that the CMC is Arcos API as you've seen in the previous slides is also applicable to other types of other devices such as cortex a devices as well. And also we're not limited to the court except for it will work with cortex M 7 and 3 m 0 0 plus and the whole family really so what it really is the CMC is are those API is like a remote controller that stands between ourselves which is our application code up here and the the artifacts operating system which is running on the actual microcontroller. So it basically provides an abstraction layer between the operating system and the application code that we the programmers write. So all the code that we will write will be written to interface with the CMC as are those API and then the CMC Sato's API will interface with the RTA ex operating system and then the RTA ex operating system we interface with the hardware. All of this is actually happening in a very efficient way because of the way it is all programmed. So it is actually very fast. And yes you will have direct access to the memory locations and the actual memory of the microcontroller in order to manipulate it directly if you want to from your application code. However the CMC is as API and the real time operating system that is going to run on the device are providing us with some higher level functionalities that we will explore later in this course and you will see how they can be very very useful when we're programming microcontrollers and embedded real time systems. So this CMC is artist API API stands for application programming interface and you can really think about it as being a remote control and it allows you to access what is inside the real power rating system using a set time and a standardized set of controls so a standardized set of functions that has been written and you only have to learn those instead of learning the intricacies of the operating system and exactly how it works and go deeper.

So it is actually the artist is actually agnostic so the the CMC is as API is artist agnostic it means that in here in your hardware it doesn't really matter whether you're running free Kratos or artifacts or any other real time operating system you prefer as long as it is compatible with the CMC as Art was API and you write your code to be compatible with the CMC are those API it will be okay. It will be able to run. Not a problem at all. Now the CMC is out of API version to provide the CMC provides CMC type wrappers for the following types of constructs so for thread management and again we will explore what threads are and how to manage them in a lot more detail throughout this course signal events mute access and semaphore So and again we will be talking about those in detail and won it by manipulating your memory pools and Qs and many more things. So these are the types of things that we are going to cover throughout this section of the court. We will explain what one of those things are and how it works and how the operating system helps you manipulate them directly.

MEMORY POOLS

Now let's talk about the concept of a memory pool and why we need them. So memory pools are thread safe memory areas. So here we have our four different threads I've asked before really and these threads perform operations on data which naturally exists in memory. Now these threads are not necessarily performing operations in specific bits of data that may be performing operations in multiple bits of data. It is possible that these operations of one thread may operate in memory locations that another thread is operating on simultaneously causing corruption of data or incorrect reading of data. Now what I should say is that unless you manipulate data from your threads in a careless manner. This would normally not happen. The operating system would normally take care of these not happening. However there are ways in which you can further control this and this is an explicit memory falling so memory lives in hardware naturally.

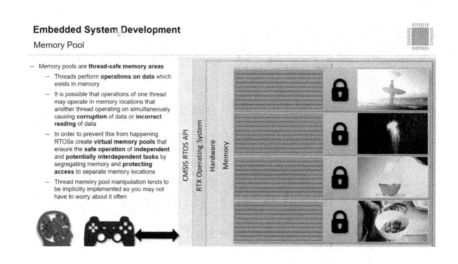

Embedded System Development

Memory Pool

— Memory pools are **thread-safe memory areas**
  — Threads perform **operations on data** which exists in memory
  — It is possible that operations of one thread may operate in memory locations that another thread operating on simultaneously causing **corruption** of data or **incorrect reading** of data
  — In order to prevent this from happening RTOSs create **virtual memory pools** that ensure the **safe operation of independent** and **potentially interdependent tasks** by segregating memory and **protecting access** to separate memory locations
  — Thread memory pool manipulation tends to be implicitly implemented so you may not have to worry about it often

CMSIS RTOS API
RTX Operating System
Hardware
Memory

Now in order to prevent this from happening so much memory in their threads using different parts of my mother that they shouldn't be using art assists real operating systems that create virtual memory pools in order to instruction of independent and potentially interdependent tasks by segregating memory and protecting access to separate memory locations. So your operating system is actually going to create some safe areas and make sure that things from one thread don't access things that another thread is using. And so on. So your operating system is doing a lot for you so you don't have to worry about it and trust me if you were trying to run to write your code to work without an operating system you would have to worry about this type of thing and it's not a fun thing to worry about. Thread memory tends to be implicitly implemented so you don't really have to worry about it very often. However on occasion you may have to worry about it. And those occasions can be cases where you are directly manipulating memory or reading something from memory mapped IO and such devices. So you have the CMC Sato's API which acts as a remote controller for you. The programmer who liked my icon for the program is here and basically through the CMC is an art API. You can actually manipulate memory. What is even more fun and we will see later on. Course what we will see is actually how you can use the operating system and actually the integration of the operating system with your integrated development environment with your IBC in order to set those balls up. It's very very interesting.

SEMAPHORES

One of perhaps the trickier and most cryptic topics in embedded systems development is a topic called simmer force. In fact the same forces are quite simple to understand that sometimes people get confused about how they work. So I am hoping to do a bit of a good job in explaining them. Given how scary they can seem to be, some of the forces are abstract constructs used to manage access to Syria reusable resources so as multiple threads of the operating systems work simultaneously they may at different times require access to a serial resource to a serial reusable resource such as an analog to digital converter. So imagine we have our outlook digital converter here and it has certain tunnels and let's imagine that we have our beautiful different operating system. We with a number of different threads around it so have thread 1 which requires access to the outlook for digital converter tunnel one third to that requires access through the ABC Channel 3 and then we have thread 3 which also requires hackers where they see tunnel one or what is actually going to happen is that if we have set things up properly the operating system is going to stop threat free from accessing tunnel one of the ABC because this tunnel is actually currently being utilized by thread 1. So third 3 is not going to access from 3 should not access it. It's quite important because a third monitor might set it to certain settings and then take a measurement and three and three might set it to certain settings and take that measurement and the settings of third three might be different from the settings of the red one. So it is possible that if we were to have both those threads manipulating the same peripheral at the same time we would cause a lot of trouble especially when you have a preemptive operating system as we have explained earlier where one thread is able to preempt the execution of another thread. So there's a lot of fun things that can actually happen here. There are two main types of force : the normal semi force and the mutual exclusion semaphore. We will look into both of those in a lot more detail. The RDX operating system is one of the operating systems that implements some of force and the CMC is out of API provides a consistent interface between the same force or the ATA ex and the programmer really. So again you get your beautiful remote control so that it doesn't matter whether it's RDX or another operating system you just learn how to write your code to utilize semaphore in the CMC artist API and then the CMC is artists API is going to take care of translating your instructions to the instructions in the language of the operating system and then the operating system is going to directly manipulate the processor and its peripherals and bring everything to you in a comprehensive API and you can use it using a beautiful remote control if you will. I'm making the remote control be your API or the API.

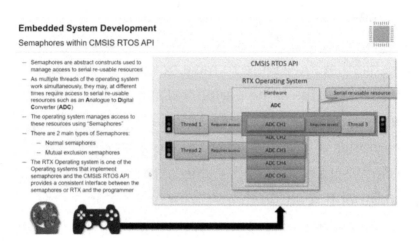

- Semaphores are abstract constructs used to manage access to serial re-usable resources
- As multiple threads of the operating system work simultaneously, they may, at different times require access to serial re-usable resources such as an Analogue to Digital Converter (**ADC**)
- The operating system manages access to these resources using "Semaphores"
- There are 2 main types of Semaphores:
  - Normal semaphores
  - Mutual exclusion semaphores
- The RTX Operating system is one of the Operating systems that implement semaphores and the CMSIS RTOS API provides a consistent interface between the semaphores or RTX and the programmer

I'm saying that it looks like a remote control for you, the programmer, so that may not make a lot of sense with respect to Semaphore, so let's try and explain some of the force in a bit more depth. So first of all we're going to examine normal semaphores as a concept that can be understood as a car park. So imagine we have a car park that has only four spaces. This car park represents a serial reusable resource. So we have only four spaces in our car park. And let's say that the equivalent example in autos could be a reusable resource which can only be used by four threads of time but not more. So let's say you have all your car. Here we have four spaces and three cars one going. So the operating system manages the resource, the semaphore and the threads where we put one car in the semaphore number. It decrements it, effectively denoting that we have one less empty space. So we've put one car in and we have three empty spaces and we move forward now and then we put another car in then we only have two empty spaces Yeah. So you're semaphore no detriments. And then again if we put the third car in we only have one empty space. So your semaphore number is 1 now. And then if a thread needs to wait before accessing a serial reusable resource vs operating system is gonna match it to so let's imagine that we have a full car park and then some other cars want to also get in.

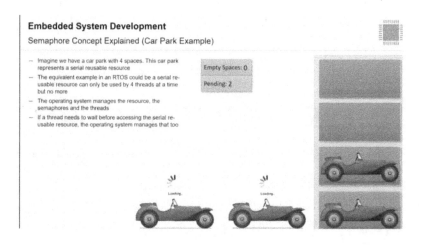

Embedded System Development

Semaphore Concept Explained (Car Park Example)

- Imagine we have a car park with 4 spaces. This car park represents a serial reusable resource
- The equivalent example in an RTOS could be a serial reusable resource can only be used by 4 threads at a time but no more
- The operating system manages the resource, the semaphores and the threads
- If a thread needs to wait before accessing the serial reusable resource, the operating system manages that too

Empty Spaces: 0

Pending: 2

Well the operating system is going to make this car wait for as long as necessary. So one of those. So we have zero empty spaces and we have one thread pending to effectively utilize zero reusable resource or one car waiting to get into the car park because the car park is full and then maybe there is another car that wants to enter the car park because the car park is still full. So our pending number is going to be increased to two of them. Yeah. Well Martin now that two of those cars leave from the car park then we have two empty spaces so we can now put those cars in so effectively the whole movement here is happening where we're left with zero empty spaces and zero Fed spending. And of course as time passes and those threads are doing their job once they finish they can release the serial reusable resource or they can release effectively their parking spot in the car park so that we can be left with her with an empty car park.

TIMERS TIMER MANAGEMENT

One of the many important features of microcontrollers are the so-called hardware timers time or specialized hardware peripherals that measure time in their roles and they're very accurate. What happens with those timers is that when you're using a timer in order to time a special operation. Actually this happens outside of the main processor so your main processor can be free to do other things while your timer is in the background measuring time timer count from zero upwards for measuring time elapsed performing a function similar to a stopwatch. They can also be used to provide time delays.

- Timers are specialised hardware peripherals that measure time intervals
  - They count from zero upwards for measuring time elapsed performing a function similar to a stopwatch
  - They can be used to provide time delays
- The hardware provides timers that are managed by the operating system
- The CMSIS RTOS API provides effectively a "remote control" for those timers which abstracts the programmer from the intricacies of the hardware

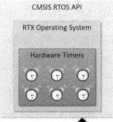

The hardware provides those times and they are monitored by the operating system so the timer certainly leaving the hardware but they are managed by the operating system RDX in our case and the CMC is our those API provides effectively a remote control for those timers which obstructs the programmer from the intricacies of actually managing the real hardware which is what happens behind the scenes.

BLINKING AN LED [AUTOMATED CODE]

This section is extremely important as we learn how to do perhaps the most important thing. An embedded software engineer ever blinks an LCD in their life. Yes my dear friends this is perhaps the most important thing we will do in this course. And if he's sort of tradition just like when you're learning C the first thing you learn to do is how to write Hello World programs. Well when you are learning embedded programming the first thing we learn to do is how to blink an eye. These are extremely easy and extremely complicated as well. It is so easy that we are going to set up this example through some ready-made piece of code that has been given to us from the developers of CMC since. So actually that's going to be very very quick. It will take less than a minute to set it up but it will take many three days to explain exactly what is going through our software. And we will see a number of different things that are happening, how it all works, how it's set up and what kinds of features of the operating system we're using. First of all though let me tell you a little small story. So there is somebody that I have worked with here in the United Kingdom who is very famous in the embedded systems community in the U.K. and actually he has written a number of books on how to use how to use these types of devices will not go any further because from what I have said you may be able to infer his name. But anyway he was sewing something once upon a time not very long ago. And he said to me well blinking early is perhaps the most important thing software engineers in the embedded systems space do. And he jokingly also said that we might as well hold a competition for whoever is going to be the person to find the most complicated and convoluted way of blinking a lady. And indeed even though the way that I'm going to demonstrate to you in this section of the course is going to be fairly simple you will see that it is actually utilizing quite a number of embedded systems concepts and it is not that simple after all. So. Well let's go about doing it then let's go set it up. First thing you want to do is you open your kind of micro vision as I have done here. You click com this button here where it says pack installer and actually give it a minute or two to load. Okay. That doesn't really need it. And what you want to do is you want to come down here for your esteemed microelectronics devices because well in this example we're going to use the board that I have on my desk which is a 32 f 4 2 9. I discovered one kit and we'll go here and actually I don't want to stay on devices. I want to go on board.

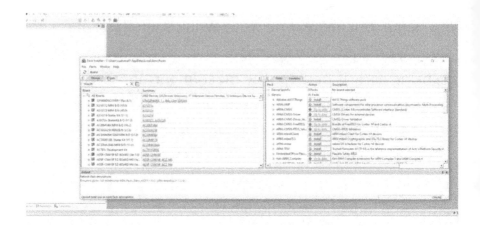

And I'm going to go on board because this is actually a place where we have a number of different examples and packet things for boards and let's search for the device such as the M 32 f 4 2 9. So this is the actual device that I have. And. Well might give you a sneak peek preview of a device that they have here blinking. So this is the one. Yep. And what we want to do really is after we have selected our device here we go to examples and what we will do is we select the first example. Sims is our toes Blinky for this board and this is we're not going to write any code here just click copy here and this is just going to copy the example from the server and into my computer and we will be able to look at the code and floss that code into the device into the board that I have connected to my computer. I'm going to show you how to do all of this stuff. So the first thing you want to do is copy and then find a reasonable location for this to go into. So this seems like a good folder for me. And if I click a K says destination folders that do not exist. You want to create it. Yes I want to create it. And it is actually going to create the files and it is actually also going to open a new instance of Kyle Micronesian with this hall with this whole cold in here. And actually what we're looking at here is an abstract text okay. This is just a little summary tells me what is the crystal clock that my system is working on and what does the system clock that my system is working on it's working at one hundred sixty eight megahertz LCD the one is blinking eyes running light with fixed speed five hundred milliseconds button.

User is used to stop or start blinking off the Libby. And again even though that looks like a very simple piece of operation this can be quite convoluted to achieve. So what I'm going to do first of all is I'm going to demonstrate to you all of the settings that I have for my S P link as stealing is actually this little piece of hardware here. This is actually the peeling tape. And what you can see here is on the left hand side. How many years has that gone to my computer? And it effectively connects to the program here and on the right hand side of the s.t. link. We have the screen now somewhere under the screen. We have the main microcontroller. Okay. And this man microcontroller is connected to and the three or these LCDs that you can see actually it's already blinking here. So yeah. So what I'm going to show you now is how to configure this as the link to the back. This is the link to tea baggers. Actually this tip here as you can see it. And the interesting thing is that these boards cover a key towards this overall development. Keep that I have bought here. It has an on board debugger so the debugger which is this tape is on board. It is possible to have a separate debugger which is a separate device. It's usually a boring gray box that says Whatever.

Well debugger it is. And then you connect it to your development kits. However this development kit has an embedded debugger and this is physically it anyway you want to do if you can come over here to this button here. So pick options for Target. And this is going to tell us okay. This is the target. You can see I have put this setting here. This is actually automatically done because the computer knows that by virtue of me telling it whatever example I'm using the computer knows whatever example I'm using and it has used the correct settings by itself as a test. It also knows that I'm using the S3 link debugger. How does it know this? Well this kit has an onboard debugger so naturally I would be using that instead of a separate debugger but anyhow this is the correct setting for this here. So when you go to debug tab you want to select as they linked debugger if this is not already selected and you can go into settings and your settings Bates should look exactly like this one what you can see here is that hey we have selected this debugger of course and it is actually using this device not really able to do anything here. Interesting part you should be here not on data but on S.W. and the rest of the settings are as follows. Here. So if you have done that here then what do you want to do is click click click click on that again. This was really pre set up for me and then what you want to do is you want to rebuild. This is going to compile and link all the files here and you can see the build log down here on my screen. So this has built everything. And then what do you want to do really is you want to load it to the device. What I'm going to do here is I'm actually going to bring this on a little bit smaller and then I'm going to bring our board here. Okay so what you're gonna say what you are and what you will see now when I click low do what you will see is that you will see that this LCD is going to start flossing and this is the communications and a working LCD of the acetate link relay and it's going to start flossing and going crazy because it's all going to be programming the main microcontroller. And after the main microcontroller has finished being programmed then we'll see only these starting to floss a little bit faster. Okay so if I'm going to click load here you can see it here on the bottom it's going really fast and you can actually see the LCD here. The LCD itself has started blinking much faster. Again not very fancy really but rather interesting.

And as we will see in the future, rather convoluted, what I'm going to do now is I'm going to use this extremely specialized button pressing instrument that I have bought and press this button here. So if I started doing this with my left hand up I would go here and press this button. Press this button you will see that the only thing that has stopped blinking and I come here again and I press this button again or is it here you will see if I press this problem again. You will see that it has started blinking again. Yeah. So in terms of functionality this example is fairly simple as you have seen. However it is utilizing quite a number of different operating system constraints which we are going to explore a lot further than that.

THREAD VISUALIZATION, FLAGS ANALYSIS

Now I do understand that the automated code for the blinky implementation is clearly the example that I showed you in the previous chapter is rather complicated. And I agree with you if you said it is what I want to do is I want to go through all the different files so mainly to see blink. You don't see and so on and explain every single bit. Okay so the first thing I want to do is I want to go through the main door to see so we're going to go through the main door to see. You can see it here. Perhaps it is better if I bring it up on a slide here. Okay. So this is an extract from mandatory so even though C is still our default entry point to the program because it is the default entry point to any C program. It does not really contain almost any of the important parts of our code. And I will explain to you why that is. So the main dot c file does a lot of the initializing and housekeeping for our application.

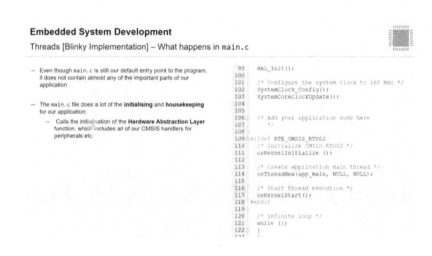

It does things such as calling the initialization and saying initialization excuse me of the hardware abstraction layer. So that's this function call up here which includes all of the CMC is hundreds for all the peripherals and it basically is the place or is the part of the code that obstructs the hardware from the operating system and the software it sets the system clock. So this is what this part does here. Now in this example we are indeed setting our system clock to one hundred sixty eight megahertz. And this is indeed the maximum system speed that this particular device that I'm using can actually achieve. It initializes the kernel of the operating system. So this is just basically starting our operating system up and in some seats the main thread of our application. So actually this is the instantiation of a thread called up Main. And this is the main thread of our application. So the main function instantiates the main thread and the main thread is actually defined somewhere else. I will show that to you very soon also starts the kernel and this is basically your scheduler. So your application is now effectively running. Yeah. This kid's really weird now schedule all the appropriate threads and allocate time to that. And with respect to when they are supposed to run and so on given their priorities and whatever. Okay. So now we're going to look at the blink. You don't see which is the other file. Now it is actually this file here. Okay. And this is where we actually find most of our code. And what you can see is inside the blink you don't see. We find this main thread void up Main so from the main dot we're actually in some skating the thread and inside this thread we do some other things.

```
68    uint32_t last;
69    uint32_t state;
70
71    for (;;) {
72        state = (Buttons_GetState () & 1U);           // Get pressed button state
73        if (state != last){
74            if (state == 1){
75                osThreadFlagsSet (tid_thrLED, 1U);     // Set flag to thrLED
76            }
77        }
78        last = state;
79        osDelay (100U);
80    }
81    }
82
83    /*----------------------------------------------------------
84     * Application main thread
85     *----------------------------------------------------------*/
86    void app_main (void *argument) {
87
88        LED_Initialize ();                             // Initialize LEDs
89        int32_t LED_Initialize()                       // Initialize Buttons
90
91        tid_thrLED = osThreadNew (thrLED, NULL, NULL); // Create LED thread
92        if (tid_thrLED == NULL) { /* add error handling */ }
93
94        tid_thrBUT = osThreadNew (thrBUT, NULL, NULL); // Create BUT thread
95        if (tid_thrBUT == NULL) { /* add error handling */ }
96
97        osThreadExit();
98    }
99
```

Now let's examine that again on the slide. So what I've brought up here is different parts of the blinky don't see file namely I've brought the three different threads that exist inside that file and I've brought some of the initialization up at the top. So in the blink you don't see we have the definition of three different threads. One of the threads is the C T H R and D. So that's the blinking MPD thread then there is another thread which checks the buttons state here and then we have the main application thread down here. So two so two of those three threads are also initially initialized. So we have three instantiations. Two initializations are three different issues to initialization. Now let's have a lo So the header files mounting the board LCD and buttons are hops included so you can see here I have Hussey included board LCD dot hates and board bottom still hates.

88

Basically these are the header files that allow our bit of code to actually connect with the different pieces of hardware. In this case it is our LCD and our board buttons. Now it should be mentioned that these Heather files are actually provided as part of the CMC arts API and it is actually part of the Harvard abstraction layer. So it seems this artist makes it very very easy for us to actually see amps is not CMC artists champs this makes it very very easy for us to get access to those only these and the buttons without having to look at the actual hardware which we will do anyway because you know it's fun and I want to sell you but we don't have to because we can get control of the LCD and the bottoms directly using those header files and the operating system and Sams is in the background is actually matching how we get access to those using with higher abstraction layer. Okay then we have this tiny tar Bath which is the thread core of a thread button which is here and this is a one thread we will look into that in more detail which is being defined and we have another thread called Tier tar LCD which is being defined here. And those two are also being declared up here. So we declare our threads and we define our threads. Okay. What else is happening the thread main up is defined as well. Remember the main up thread is actually being defined here. Here's the definition. However it has been instantiated in the main door to file. Okay so now within the up Main. So within this place up here down here what do we have? We have the LCD being initialized. So this is a function that initializes our realities and basically connects them internally in our operating system so we can use them. We have the initialization of the buttons. You can see I live in the UK and that this code was written for American standards so they use that. I use them both correctly. It's just different spelling threads t it's our button t it's our only these are instantiated so I am instantiating those two threads and here is the instantiation of each one of those rights. So here is the declaration of T I'd be P H R D. So that's the declaration of the thread. This is the definition of the thread in this is the instantiation of a thread like right.

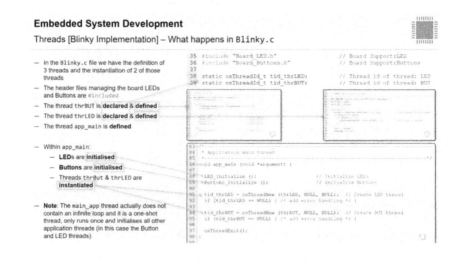

What is important to note is that the main up thread actually does not contain an infinite loop and that it is a one shot thread. It only runs once from top to bottom and at the other end it initializes all other application threads so it runs once and then it exits. Now all other threads that I have initialized here actually H are only the integrator but if these two threads are actually going to run in an infinite loop they have an infinite loop inside them and. Well I can prove that to you they are just going in here and we can look inside a t h r but so that's the bottom thread and you can see it has an infinite loop. How do we know it's in an infinite loop? It starts with 4 and then two semicolons here. So that's like an infinite loop. Yeah it will just keep running forever. Now one of the first things that we need to understand is how signal events are operating. So let's look at the principles of their operation: a signal event is a notification of some event having taken place; signals have originators and receptors otherwise known as senders and receivers in rocket science. Yet here they are used to communicate between different threads so you can tell from one thread to another thread that an event has taken place. Basically, synchronous or asynchronous threads can choose which signals they monitor and what action is taken when one of those signals is triggered. So you can imagine we have a number of threads here and this thread is monitoring those three signals. This thread is monitoring those for signals and this thread is one through those three signals and you can imagine that there is some sort of complex relationship between them.

Basically what thread monitors would signal and so on now all those signals and threads and events are minors inside the artifacts operating system and all of those can be accessed using the CMC archives API which is what we've been using throughout this course. So let's imagine that we have read one and thread two so we have two independent threads. So let's say that thread 2 is running and it's doing its thing and then at some point it arrives at some place and it says well I got to wait a bit here because I'm waiting for something what am I waiting for. Well it is actually waiting for a signal. Okay so the third two are waiting for a signal. It just so happens that at some point third one does something and that something that happened inside thread one causes a signal to be produced and that signal is the same signal that is being received by thread 2 so effectively thread 1 is sending a signal to thread 2 Yeah. So at this point the third two can stop waiting. Yeah it doesn't need to wait anymore. And what it will do is it will run and it will do its thing and then it will come back to the beginning. Hearings will start the whole cycle again and then it will wait to get the signal again. Then it can run again once the signal comes again. So this is basically the very simple operation of signals. Simple as it might look right here. It's slightly more complicated when you look at it in the actual code.

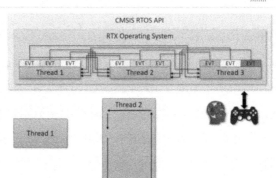

- A signal event is a notification of some event having taken place
- Signals have originators and receptors (senders and receivers)
- Are used to communicate between different threads
- Can be synchronous or asynchronous
- Threads can choose which signals they monitor and what action is taken when each one of those signals is triggered
- All threads and signals are managed in a structured way by the operating system
- The CMSIS RTOS API provides a standardised interface between the programmer and the operating system

Okay so this is our only D thread. Okay so you remember we have the button thread and the lady thread. This is the lady thread. And basically inside the lady thread we have this bit of code here. So let's try and explain that bit of code because it's interesting. Very interesting indeed. Remember this one was auto generated. This is an example. Yeah it's an example code. So first of all we have a declaration of a local variable active flag which is one you well first of all not one you use doesn't really mean anything. Well it does mean that it is unsigned and it is mandated from me as. So this you is actually required means receipt. 2004 rule ten point six which says that the suffix U S be applied to all constants of unsigned type and because the wanted to follow the MEs Rousey rules for creating the operating system and CMC is in general they had to put this u there because they're following the set of rules. Well it all it does is it really means it is an unsigned integer. Yeah don't worry too much about it just really that's the number one really. Okay so now that I've answered this potential question that you may have, let's have a look at what happens here. So first of all I would declare an unsigned integer which is called Active underscore flag and we set it to 1 and it's an integer of 32 bits and then we have an infinite loop. This infinite loop starts here. Okay. And it starts here and it finishes power here. All right. Now let's look a bit further. So this first if statement in here all it would do is really if there was a signal and that was equal to the number one then it would be toggling the flag. I have a problem here face to face because actually we have two separate uses for the word flag in these very two lines. Actually we have one variable of which we can toggle to make it either one or zero in order to tell us if the button has been pressed or not. And then we have another thing called a flag which is the name of the signal function from the actual thread. It's a total mess. Okay. So basically if the button is pressed then this bit of code here is going to run and then we will compare this to the number one and if it is one. So if a button husband pressed and it is a one then what we will do is we will talk to the variable called active flag. So this flag here and this flag here actually have nothing to do with each other. It's just an unfortunate name that they're both called flags really okay not we got that out of the way. What we do is okay. So as I said this is a live statement. All it really does is to toggles the flag. And I will show you exactly how it toggles the flag on the next

94

slide. But for now just keep in your mind that it doubles the flag. So if a certain function called always thread flags wait returns one that is this function here always red flags wake if it returns one then we take the variable called active flag and perform this operation to it. Now when we perform this operation to it so you can see this operation here. All it does is it really topples the flag. So this is basically the actual functionality and it works as follows. All it really does is it targets the variable if it is a one then it makes the zero. And if it is a zero then it makes it the one I said again on the next slide that will explain exactly how this works if the flag is raised. When I say the flag is raised I mean if the flag is equal to one then it means that the button has been pressed or effectively we have given a command for the entity to blink. So we do the blinking only and wait a bit and turn it off. Wait a bit. Yeah. And then I would go back up again throughout the loop again to check the bottom. Say here's the button being pressed if the button hasn't been pressed and do nothing if the button husband pressed and told me the flag and if.

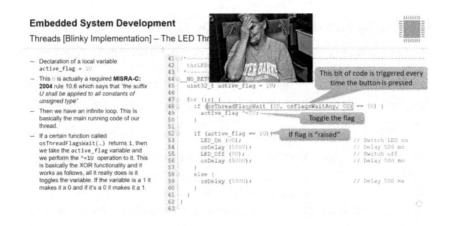

- Declaration of a local variable active_flag = 1U
- This U is actually a required **MISRA-C: 2004** rule 10.6 which says that *'the suffix U shall be applied to all constants of unsigned type'*
- Then we have an infinite loop. This is basically the main running code of our thread.
- If a certain function called osThreadFlagsWait(...) returns 1, then we take the active_flag variable and we perform the ^=1U operation to it. This is basically the XOR functionality and it works as follows, all it really does is it toggles the variable. If the variable is a 1 it makes it a 0 and if it's a 0 it makes it a 1.

```
41 /*------
42    thrLED
43  *-----
44 __NO_RET
45    uint32_t active_flag = 1U;
46
47    for (;;) {
48        if (osThreadFlagsWait (1U, osFlagsWaitAny, 0U) == 1U) {
49            active_flag ^=1U;
50        }
51
52        if (active_flag == 1U) {
53            LED_On (0U);                // Switch LED on
54            osDelay (500U);             // Delay 500 ms
55            LED_Off (0U);               // Switch off
56            osDelay (500U);             // Delay 500 ms
57        }
58        else {
59            osDelay (500U);             // Delay 500 ms
60        }
61    }
62 }
63
```

This bit of code is triggered every time the button is pressed

Toggle the flag

If flag is "raised"

And then text is the flag said to one well if the flag is set to 1 then blink the LCD ones and come back around the loop. So that's how it really works. And here we have a delay. So if they if your bottom hasn't been pressed or if the flag is not raised or if effectively only the blinking is off if you will then we will not be pushing. Then we will not be running this thread. We will not run it and we will not be running this bit of code rather what will we be doing who is running the L statement and that's just an operating system delay. So just wait half a second and then go back up the loop. So in and in whichever case this thread is going to have a delay either using or using this buff. So if the flag is activated who will be using an hour's delay here that's a half a second. That's half a second. Again this is doing your lady blinking and if the flag is not activated then who will still be waiting for the coffin second before we go back up and re-evaluate the condition of the thread. So we've built in some and some delay that is not to hog the process or at all times. And here I say Else wait a bit and try again. Yeah. That's what it does. So this is how this whole thread works really. So again what this thread does is declares a variable, calls it active flag then and and then the infinite loop begins in that infinite loop. It first starts the questions. The question has the button being pressed. If the button has been pressed then what we do is we toggle the flag and then we take the flag raised. Yes if the flag is raised then blank the entity if the flag is not raised then wait a little bit and then do the same whole thing again from beginning to end. Yeah. So this whole infinite loop is all right. So I did promise to you that I will explain to you how this toggling the flag works. So how did this strange looking operator come here? So let's go and have a look at it. Exactly. First of all this is the X or functionality and I'm going to explain how the extra functionality works and how the compound operators work. Okay. So what we have here is we have X equals three y equals two. So we've got two decimal numbers here. I'm going to write them down as binary. So this is the number three in binary that's the number two in binary. And what I'm going to do is I'm going to x all of them. Now X ordering yields a result that is saying basically if either one of the two bids that I'm comparing is a one then I'm going to give a 1 however are both of one or both a zero. I'm going to give a zero so one X or zero is one obviously but one X or one is going to be zero. And then of course there are actual 0 0 0 6 0 0 0. But actually our example is much more simple than that. So first of all let me show you the basic operation of this compound. Operator. This is called a compound assignment operator. Okay. That is to say this statement here X equals X plus 3. That's exactly the same thing as x plus equals 3 okay. So what does it do then? Well this statement what did we do. The order of execution here is that the first thing that will happen is the X will be added to the number three. So we will take the X whatever X contains, maybe x contains then yeah and we will add it to the number three and then we will get a result. And then what we will do with this result is we will assign it to X.. So X will stop being then it will become 13. Let's say we have X being ten. Okay so it will be 10 plus three that the number 13 number 13 goes and sits up here. And then what we do is we do the assignment operator and then this goes from here to here. I do have a c course where this is explained in much more detail actually exactly how this works inside the computer so we can look it up on my profile if you wish right. And that doing this operation here is precisely the same as writing x plus equals 3. So x plus equals 3 is shorthand for writing this in the same manner X star equals 3 is shorthand for writing this and X Ampersand equals 3 is shorthand for writing this and of course X X or 3 is shorthand for writing this so in the previous slide when you saw this notation. Yeah a sort of up arrow and equals. That's what we really meant, that's the principle. That's the basic principle of operation. So let's look at this God again. This is the part that we have in question.

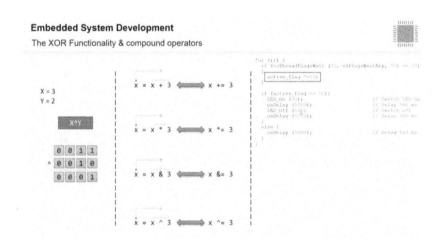

Embedded System Development

The XOR Functionality & compound operators

Now remember this was originally said to be a one so I go back to my quote up here and I go up here you can see here inserted to underscore the active flag is actually or is not set to be a one. Okay right. So let's say that. Well first of all it is actually a 32 bit integer. How do we know this? Well it says thirty two underscore T. So that's a 32 bit integer type. And it is unsigned. How do we know it's unsigned? Well it says here you. And then whatever we put inside it is also one year which is also again unsigned. Of course. All right so let's get back to this. So it's a 32 bit integer and it's a 32 bit integer which has the number one inside it. That's what it is by default. Now if we were to do that statement what we would do effectively is if we were to run that statement. So if that statement of value is right to true and we were to run that statement to condemn the situation that we would have is the following we would have a 1 x AUD with a 1 if you x or a 1 with a 1 What do you get. Well you get a zero. Yeah. We'll explore that here. And that's what you do if you x or one with a one you get a zero. So basically what this statement does is it explores the current value of the variable with the number one and it saves the result of that operation back into that variable. Now if we had a zero originally and we explored it within one so in the opposite case effectively then zero x or one is going to be a one.

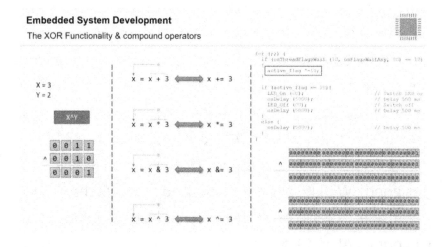

Embedded System Development

The XOR Functionality & compound operators

So this statement effectively takes whatever this variable is and toggles it if it's a zero it will make it a one if it's a one. It will be zero. This is why I'm saying it toggles it like a straight. Yeah it's a one it makes zero zero it makes it a one. And this is how it works in the background now the next thing I wanted to show you is how the bottom thread works. Now I warn you that this is a very boring thread. Now why is it a very boring firm? Well it doesn't really do math. So in the blanket you c file we have the definition of three threads in the instantiation of two of those threads. One of those threads is the bottom thread. The other one is the lady's thread. Those are the two that are instantiated and they are instantiated in the main thread. I'll show you that later on but basically now let's focus on the bottom thread. So this is the bottom thread. Here is all the code for it. And all it really does is it gets the state of the bottom after what it first creates. Those two are local variables that it has one of them is called Lost the other one is called state and only rarely does it and it does it in an infinite loop as you can see it here in the infinite loop. It does get the state of the bottoms it I'm sort of with the variable one and there is one why does that is because it needs to only with the value of one button. And it takes that whole thing and it puts that inside the state. I remember the state is itself a variable I'm signed into 0 32 bits. Now if the state is not what it used to be. So if the state of the bottom is different from what it was. Now what it does is it sets the flag. Actually that arrow should be up here. Yeah it sets the flag. Now the moment this flag is set what happens is the operating system understands it says oh the flag is set so every time the lady's thread says it was my flag I said what the operating system will come here. So well it was set by this threat at some point. So yes. Yeah. And that would actually be handled by the operating system. Now otherwise what it does is it waits hundreds milliseconds and then it repeats. And that's why I'm saying it's a very boring thread. It really doesn't happen once. It just checks if the button is the same as the buttons. Hate is the same as it was. And if it is the same as it was. If the bottom state is not the same as it was then it. What it does is it sets a flag and then the other thread picks up that signal of the flag. Having been said, it does its own thing which we have explored in the previous slides.

LED BUTTONS DRIVERS HARDWARE

So far we have examined a number of the aspects of these code examples here called the blinky LCD. Yep. And what I think is probably a good idea to show you is. Well I suppose the only blinking since I've promised to you that is blinking so here it is. And you can see the end is actually blinking.

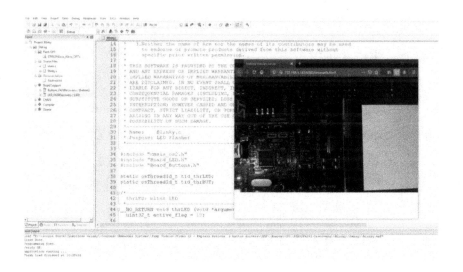

Let me see whether I can turn off the flashlight here and you can see it blinking more beautifully. Just focus again. So here it is you can see the LRT is really actually proper deliberate blinking. OK so let's have a look at exactly how our code here in the blinky dot see file is actually making this entity blink down here so gonna put that only on the side first of all. And we really want to understand. Okay. This is the ease of bringing it back. This really exists on a printed circuit board and it's connected somehow to the processor as a good software and hardware and embedded hardware and software engineer. You really need to have an understanding of how your eye from your bit of code to actually looking at this lady blinking and you'd really need to have a bit of an understanding of what your hardware looks like. So there is this file called well can see it. Here it is. Basically the discovery kit user manual and inside the Discover kit user manual which is this big document that I'm looking at here and I have a link to it on the course so that you can find it. So I will have attached to this file with your with this video you can actually see the proper schematics of the discovery kit. And actually if you wanted to zoom in here, what you will see is that we have the green LCD which LTE, which was called LTE three last month, Matic and it connects to port PD 13 on our processor.

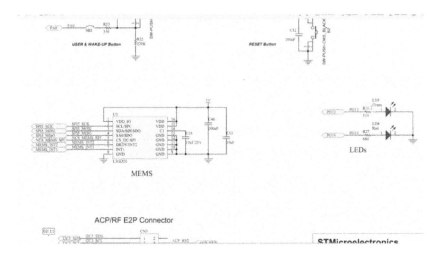

So this actually directly goes to P.G. 13 on our processor
and if. Well if I wanted to go and see the ports of the
processor you can see the person has port A port B port C
and port the. And they should have port T. Now for the
14. Okay. So from Port G 14 here it goes directly to our
only D connection. It actually goes to a resistor of 26 and
then to our LCD. Yeah. And actually if I was to bring that
back up here you will see that it says here. Okay P G
thirteen and these three are 26. So they are physically
located close to each other as well. So the resistance
physically close to reality it doesn't really matter where it
physically is but they so happen to be close to each other
and you can imagine that the truck from here from that
resistor goes actually to what the processor is but if you
cannot see it going because it's on a different layer on the
ECB I imagine. Okay so now that we have discussed a little

bit about that let's see how our software can really interpret that. So first of all you can see actually there is another entity here more PDC Fortran which is a red entity. So what we're going to try and do is we're going to try and blink their ability instead of the green entity. So the first thing I want to show you is okay let's go to the end of the thread and you can see here we have this statement called Only the on the off.

Now somehow this early on and only the off functions find their way through our operating system down to the hardware and then they make the of the Blinking so this only the on is actually a function which is defined here. Well you can right click and say go to definition but what it will do is it will not do us a favor of going through a definition but actually you can see here we have included board LCD dot hates. Now if I go to the board only to hate, I can actually right click that and say Open Document and that's going to open the document okay. And you can see that this function early on is defined here but it is not declared here. Yeah. So while it is declared here, it's beautiful. But let's see what we can find about its actual definition. Well it turns out that this whole board that we have got here okay has full support from our operating system and it's got all of the hardware abstraction layers all of those are already existing in our system. So basically what I can do is I can go to the board support package here. So here on the left hand side I see board support. I can double click on these LCD board support files okay. So this is the file that actually creates the hardware abstraction layers for the NLD for this particular board that I have here. Okay. And basically this is provided from a steam microelectronics app as you can see here. So this is provided by Steve and this is basically so that they can make our life easier for programming that device and you can see here actually that the LCD on LG on function is defined here. Okay. Now what I'm gonna do is I'm not going to spend too much time looking at exactly how this and the on function works. However what you will remember is that actually there is this LCD called also Aldi for which is a reality and we remember that because we saw that on our schematic. Okay. So what I want to do is I want to see whether instead of the green light the air can start more I can modify my code to blink theoretically. So all I really need to do is say well what I can do is I should be able to go to they said blink. You don't see the file here containing the argument of not only the function but the answer instead of telling it to turn on the LCD zero. I'm going to tell it to turn on the LCD one and hear the same again. So I'm gonna bring this up here.

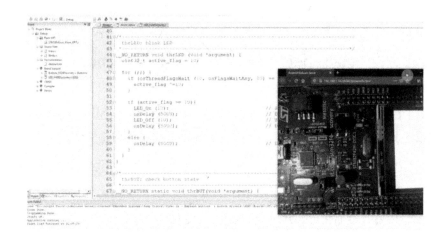

Make half my screen here. This and the other half there so you can see exactly what I'm doing. So if I'm going to recompile all of my code here and then download it to the board we'll see that now instead of the green blinking we have the right blinking if you wanted to be really fancy what you could do is you could have of these blinking green and red like that's what I'm going to do here so I'm just notifying my code so that it links both the LCD and the one off levy zero off as well so that you will see now when I loaded onto the board and loading it into board you see this lady going crazy and then you can see those two blinking. Yeah and while I suppose uh I could also mix it up a bit if I really wanted to so switching off one while turning on the other yeah. Let this get itself useful at the moment I messed it up rudely and what I'm going to do here to download this here. So I'm off to mix them up. Yeah. Another fun thing you can do is modify this number from operating system delay later. It says here is half a second from on to off. So what I'm gonna do is I'm gonna make that perhaps two hundred milliseconds so point to a second. Just make things a little bit quicker and hopefully my camera should be able to sort to use some flushing this code in and yeah. So we're making it to floss faster basically. Yeah. And if you want to be really fancy I'll make it one so. Think about complicated ways of flushing and these well you can see flashing I can see flashing cameras all that bother picking it up actually. So yeah you can see that our ladies are blinking which is well. Woo hoo. That's what I'm better at. Blaine Kelly these basics are just very complicated finding very complicated ways of thinking about this. So I'm just gonna return our calls to their original state here So basically our example has broad support and aid has got all the support basically for the ladies on the board already. Now this also the reason why this happens is because the SD as I said has made this board and they want people to use it so they have already created this example that I've shown you how to download and run on your computer and on your board and they have also sold us how to. Well they've also created this board support file. Now if you're buying different boards then you will. You are more than likely to find those board support files that will plug into this. This bit of code. Now why. What is special about CMC s.

CMC is a standardized way of interfacing. Your board support files effectively to your code so that all the interfaces are standardized so the manufacturers write all of their board support files and the hardware abstraction layers in a way that they speak to the hardware and CMC is and then you write your own code which is this blank you don't see file effectively to speak to CMC is and therefore we are using this middle layer which is called CMC so in order to interface everything to it as you have seen on the previous slides and this is why CMC is very useful and uh well it really is capable of saving you huge and huge and huge amounts of time. Now talking about the board support packet there are also board support packets from the bottoms. Now there's only a couple of bottoms freely on this board and you can see them here. We have the reset button and it goes to their recent Spin of the microcontroller. So we're not going to press that or I am going to press that and show you how it works. And we've got the they say user and wake up button and it's got some circuitry around it. I'm going to go through the circuitry here but basically this is the user button that toggles on and off our LCD whether they would be operating or not. OK so it says here the button is called Yeah but the button a said the user button. Now what I'm going to show you is what happens if I press this button so you can see here this is actually the user button you can see it here. I'm going to use my other special button pushing instrument that they have here called my finger because it's easier and you can see that when I push this button the entity will stop flashing so actually you can see the stop flashing push the button I push it again starts flashing again I push it again stops flashing. Now what I could do is I could push the other button. The reset button has a black button up here. If I push the reset button that's going to reset the whole system and at the end it is going to start flashing again. So it's a threat to the system and it was very quick to wake up so early they started flashing again. What happened there. Now let me show you the blinky example here. The blinky dots example is actually looking at the bottom using that thing called the threat button. Yeah. So in this thread here we can see that button and we can check whether the button has been pressed so here we have this thing called button get state. Okay. And this is getting the state of the button basically as they said and one here is just clearing all the other bits of that port and just making sure that we get only the button here so it can get the state of the button and actually again if I was to tell it to take me to the definition it will deny. However what I can do is I can actually go here board bottoms and open this file and that's going to open the header file and that header file has all the declarations for things such as buttons get state to get the state of the button and actually this get state of the button is defined in here in that headboard support file called bottom's EF 4 2 9 discovery which is basically the name of our board dot C. And this is where all the code for actually the definition of getting the state of the button is and you can see does a number of things here. I'm not going to go very deep into what every bit of this code does not right now anyway. Yeah but this is the bottom get state function and it goes to the hover obstruction layer and it reads GPI O port. And it returns something not gonna get into any more detail than this actually what I want to do is effectively if you click this plus button here it actually shows you every single header file that this c file is looking at. Yeah. And you can see it's looking at the hardware abstraction layer files it is looking at the hardware obstruction Blair files here it's looking at this how file it's looking at this how file it's looking at this how file and actually this this when I click the plus here it doesn't only bring me those two Header files but it brings me the header files that these Heather files are also pointing to. OK so it brings you all of the dependency tree up here. That's very useful. Works really seriously nicely. So I compile all of my code. You can see it compiles nicely again and there's nothing really anything here to show you. There's not nothing more here. So you. But this was just to make you understand what this board support layer does.

DEBUGGING SINGLE STEPPING

First of all I'll tell you a little story. So back in the good old days of computers that were seriously big so talking about computers that were physically the size of a room and perhaps a bigger room where the transistors instead of being extremely small in the order of nanometres inside they ICP you that they would be actually physical transistors or physical big lumps. Yeah like hey you have some transistor radios if you've seen so this type of thing is really really big things. So back in those days maybe you would have some cockroaches or some other bugs in the room where the computer was seized. You may find that an actual proper bug is actually causing some issues with your program not running properly because perhaps a cockroach has been stuck in some mechanical or other part or electrical part of your system so you'd have to do actual proper debugging. Of course it has ever since been adopted to a bag being some sort of trouble with your piece of software and debugging being the action of making sure that you have removed all of those things called bugs from your software.

Modern compilers and integrated development environments such as the one we are currently using have these bugs that are integrated into the overall system and these can be run independently on the tool or they can actually be run in conjunction with some sort of connection to the actual target which is what we have in our system here. We actually have a proper connection to our target. This is the target by the way. And this is the onboard debugger if you will. So yeah it's quite interesting and a lot of fun. We will talk about it now. What is actually possible to do is it is possible to single step through each line of our code as it executes on the hardware in real time and see what happens inside the hardware. So let's try and do that. Well first of all I am going to share with you all of my debugger settings. I have done this already earlier on in this course. However we will do this again. So I'm going to just click on this button here and go to where it is targeted so you can see the settings that they have here. These were indeed the default settings. I didn't have to touch anything here and there. If you go to work to debug, I'm using the Asti link debugger because actually this development kit here is coming from SD and it has the actual link debugger here. This actual tape is the SDK linked by your SO. And it is directly connected from and taking signals from the micro USB that is here. Well it's actually many uses. Technically speaking from the mini USB that is here and it connects to the main processor somewhere under here. And anyway if you go to the settings of the debugger you will see here that a tenth. Well I've cut that 10 megahertz of clock for trigger communication instead of a tag here and a clock is 168 megahertz. I have not an A I that has not enabled trace. We'll talk about traces. That's all there is to it. You will see here that I'm actually using the algorithm for a 1 megabyte device.

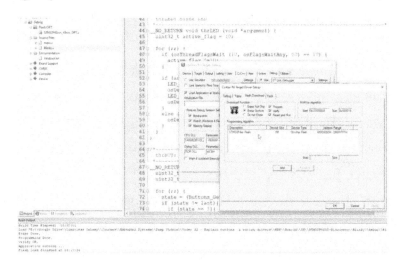

Floss while indeed the device that we're actually using is two megabytes. I'm going to leave these here for now. This may not be the best option but I am going to leave this now because this was the default option and here is however something has been set up just in case yours doesn't work. Some showing you how mine works all the settings so that you can make sure that you have all the same settings. So something else really here apart from clicking this button here. So let's build our code once again so you can see it's all built and nice. And what we're going to do is download it on to on the device as well and he will bring that device here so that you can see it so you can see the device running the code quite happily and what we can do here now is I'm going to enter debug mode so by clicking on this button I enter debug mode. And click on that and that enters the back mode. So right now you can see my code has not started running yet. OK so I have not started running yet. However, what we can do. Well first of all I want to make this window smaller so we can fit a little bit more of the code on the screen here And actually the only part that we are interested in seeing is the LCD so bringing that micro level is smaller here. Good. So here what we've got we've got this reset option so we can actually reset the microcontroller for a click that addresses the microcontroller. Now it's not doing anything very interesting because while Atari sets it up it does not actually start the program and it is possible for me to start the program running. So if I click this button here I will see that the entity will start blinking. So I've started running the program. You will see that the LCD started blinking.

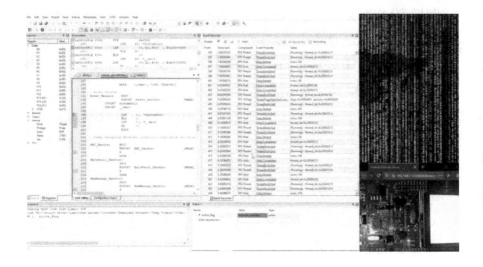

What is quite interesting you will see here in the event recorder that I have started actually recording all of the ever all the events that the operating system is going through so we can see that at this time from the beginning of this event is happening and it is actually the delay or thread streets or something like this so you will see here you can see here that how your processor is running and everything that your operating system is actually doing is being reported here. So every time you have a threat on the streets then this is recorded here and so on. Interestingly enough if you go to debug and operating system support you can choose to have something called the system. So I'm going to go there for the third year. Now I'm sorry. And the reason why I'm sorry is that this does not work. Now I was banging my head against the wall for hours to figure out why it doesn't work. So what you will find is that the system and threat of your only supports Kyla x four point eight or earlier and basically we're running out takes five. So what country has that? So you can then use the component viewer and you end up with something that looks like this so actually what you can do is you can go here and you can go to view system view and you go to a system of your and then you can see a number of things including what was I RDX excited to see go to watch windows RDX artists and that's going to give you a view of what is happening on the operating system so you can see here. We have a number of threads running. This is an idea Fred. This is the time or thread and we have the LCD thread and the button running on our system and it gives you also the stock fuses and you can actually expand on that and you can see whether we have delays, time outs and other things here.

So you can actually look into your operating system and a number of its attributes. Now what's even more fun is that you can actually single step further code. So this is a Windows event. Your system and thread of yours just don't work because we're running our takes five so if you've been used to going here or support and go to the system I heard you're well sorry just don't work now the event recorder still works. So what we can actually do here is we can stop our code and instruct by putting a breakpoint that sees a little red circle next to a certain line of code called a break. Fine so if I put a breakpoint in the place where we turn on the LCD you will see that the code will stop next time the LCD turns on or just before the LCD is known. And then if I go in here and step over that go to the next line then you will see that the LCD should turn on you. So if I go to the next line of code the lady has not turned on. Then if I press that button again. So step over let's go and around half second delay and then we'll go to the next line so trying this half a second delay what the next line and then it will turn off and then it will run half a second delay and then if we go back up here it will say Okay we've been having it changed because nobody push the button. And then we go off here so you can actually single step through the code. Okay. Or at any point your bored single stepping from the code you can press this around button and will run OK so another fun thing you can actually do here is uh let's put a breakpoint here. So if I click here on you will see that this bit of code never actually gets executed because we never actually since we're not pushing the button or not hitting this. This place here. I want to push the button. What you will see is that we are going to hit this. Push the button. Now push the button and our code has a month to get here. OK because I post about them. So this signal was effectively triggered and I've come here. So what I've actually done here is modified this variable so I'm going to toggle it. If it wasn't one I will make the zero and if it was a zero I will make it at one. So what I can do is I can actually select right click on it and I click here where it says add active flag to watch one. So this is a watch window on what has happened here as I was well I actually just run it before I'm David Fisher So I've got it twice if I click delete it will just keep it once if I click it again it will remove all the variables that I have there I can add it again I'm adding it to watch one and what this is actually going to do is it actually going to monitor this variable in real time in the memory of the microcontroller and display what it sows. Well I created this variable here on my screen so it's a one and it cannot evaluate now because we're running through the whole code, insults really going in there to see it again. But what I can actually do here is Remember it was a one if I click the button again it will become a zero. Let's see I made it into a zero. OK I've made it into a zero and if I run the code again you will see the LCD blinking now and if I click the button again I will turn it into a one yeah I've turned it into a one. And even if I click for the code to keep running you will see that the LCD is not turning on in fact it's not turning on or off and it follows to understand that this bit of code is not running here because the flood is not set to 1 and the flag is indeed at 0 so actually what I'm going to do is if I put a breakpoint here here here we should not be hitting those breakpoints at all. Yeah but if I were to breakpoint here we should be hitting that breakpoint and sure enough we have hit that breakpoint Okay ok because it was the election the else condition of that if statement that actually the next time around the loop we're going to hit that again we're going to hit that again until somebody thinks I'm gonna remove that breakpoint from their and if I going to hit the if I'm going to press the button or hit here and there we'll see that variable will change. That was set to 1. Now this. If we lift the if statement we're about 8 to 1 then we're gonna turn on white turn off weight and so on. That is extremely valuable for this breakpoint capability because you can actually monitor live what is happening to different memory locations. How do you do that? Select the variable that you want.

You right click on it and you go to add to watch one or two watch two is actually two different watch windows that you can have here and you can actually go here and watch your variables. It tells you what type of the variable is and what the contents of that variable are. In this case it displays it in hexadecimal. So it's really really useful. You can actually Toggling it so it displays it in decimal but by default is hexadecimal. I actually prefer to be hexadecimal so this is a little bit of debugging for you. And what are some of the capabilities that you actually have with your software here. Are the things you can do as you can actually come here to the view and what you can do is you can go to the system view or here and you can actually monitor your different very ferals if you have SBI. And if you have SBI your art. If you're using your USP you can monitor those. If you have other things I want to see your GPO. Now remember this is PDC 13. So let's go and monitor for our GPO port deal. If I'm monitoring Port de from our mighty GPI. Oh okay. And you should be able to see Okay here we go. You can actually see Port de 14 PDC 14 is actually Spain is being toggled up and down.

THINGS YOU MUST KNOW

Now let's talk about you, things you must know before moving forward. First, you need to know what an embedded system is and what the system is. Basically a computer system with dessicated functions within a larger electromechanical system. They range from simple portable devices like wearables and PS3 players, etc., up to large, complex systems like automotive, telecommunications and other applications. Now, when it comes to microcontrollers. It's basically a small computer, a single integrated circuit. It includes the processor memories and input output peripherals called pieces on an embedded system. Now, you might find these computer systems on cars, on, let's say, motherboards or satellites and on any PC.

Now, let's talk about a few terms that you need to know about in the A, R or R architecture. It's basically a set of suffocations regarding the instruction set, execution model, glimmery organization, instruction cycle and more, which describes a machine. Implementing that architecture on Cortex is basically a wide set of 30 to 64 are architectures. The first one on the list is Cortex A, it stands for applications designed for hosting rich operating system platforms like Linux, Android, etc.. There is also cortex, and it stands for embedded processors optimized for the empted market, low cost, energy efficient and low power. There is also cortex ah, which is real time, high performance and very critical scenarios, reliability, real time response, and, for example, the automotive world where we need zero real time applications.

STMicroelectronics and the STM32 platform

- **STMicroelectronics** is a French-Italian multinational electronics and semiconductor manufacturer headquartered in Geneva, Switzerland.

- **STM32** is a family of 32-bit microcontrollers developed by STMicroelectronics. Based on the 32-bit ARM processor cores. Specifically, in the ARM Cortex-M architecture.

- In particular, we work in this course with the **STM32 microcontroller** which belongs to the family of low-power microcontrollers.

- The STM32 MCU is placed within the **Nucleo development board**. The Nucleo boards provide a medium for debugging and development with the microcontroller units.

Now, you might hear about are holding or arm holding, which is a British company that develops the architecture of arm based products, its intellectual property business model, and it's a very famous company nowadays. Now, let's also talk about fuel terms regarding the storm or as the micro-electronics and the Estienne 32 platform. ASTM, or microcontrollers, is a French Italian multinational electronics and semiconductor manufacturer headquartered in Geneva, Switzerland. ASTM 32 is a family of 32 bit microcontrollers developed by Estie Micro-electronics based on the 32 bit arm processor cores, specifically in the arm cortex and architecture. In particular, we work in this course with the STEM 32 microcontroller, which belongs to the family of low power microcontrollers, that's the answer to MCU being placed within the Nuclear Development Board. Then boards provide a medium for debugging and development with the microcontroller units. These are the main terms that you need to know before moving forward with this, cause I hope that everything is now clear. You need to understand what an impetus system is, what a microcontroller is.

THE WORLD OF STM

Is that cortex, m3 core? M stands for Embedded System, this is an open world of armed standard called. Now, what comes next is the perforates basically provides high performance and low power, high level of integration, innovation in development, which helps you start connecting anything to your bauk. The product range is the next level. It has a family fully and in peripherals and software compatible that will help you rationalize your development.

The World of STM32

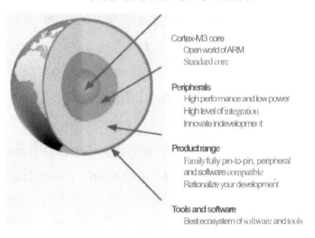

Cortex-M3 core
Open world of ARM
Standard core

Peripherals
High performance and low power
High level of integration
Innovate in development

Product range
Family fully pin-to-pin, peripheral
and software compatible
Rationalize your development

Tools and software
Best ecosystem of software and tools

The last thing is tools and software, provided it has the best ecosystem of software and tools and we will discover this as we go in this course. So whenever you see a.T.M 32 system, you need to consider these four things. The call will be the cortex, M3 or Cortex A or any other cortex core. It will be connected to peripherals and it usually provides a wide variety of product range. It also has tools and software that will help you develop things easily and debug in no time.

KEY FEATURES

Let's talk about the key features for an hour, 32 bit cortex and three core Flash and Isaura. Now, this court M3 core has up to 512 kilobyte flash memory and up to 64 kilobyte Esraa, it supports clock reset and supply management. It has multiple communication peripherals like Eye to see us Erste S.P.I. Now, it also supports sleep, stop, stand by, low power mode. It has multiple, 16 bit timers, which means that you can use more than one timer and they are all 16, which is a very good feature. It's a personal time clock, the air controller and 12 bed digital to analog converter. It also has an easy development phase and fast time to market.

Key Features

- ARM 32-bit Cortex"-M3 core with embedded Flash and SRAM
  - ☐ Up to 512KB Flash memory
  - ☐ Up to 64KB SRAM
- Clock, reset and supply management
- Multiple communication peripherals
  - IC, USART, SPI
- Sleep, Stop and Standby low power mode
- Multiple 16-bit timer
- Real-time clock
- DMA controller
- 12-bit DAC
- Easy development, fast time to market

So you can start the development process today. And a week from now, you can release your product to market as it has a lot of development software that will help you debug and develop your code easily. These are some of the features that codecs M3 corps supports. Now there are other calls with more features, but depending on your specific application, you can go and find the one that works for you. But we are just getting started.

APPLICATIONS

When it comes to a state I'm 32 or cortex applications, you can find them everywhere. Regarding the industrial application, you can find a lot of policies that are based on steel and our architecture, you can find inverters, printers, scanners and industrial networking. When it comes to building and security, you can find a lot of alarm systems, video intercom, H.V. AC systems that are built or built on our architecture and the cortex. Um. Gore, there are also the low power applications you can find in a lot of applications like glucose meters, power meters, battery operated applications, as it's called, low power mode.

Applications

Industrial:
- ✓ **PLC**
- ✓ Inverters
- ✓ Printers, scanners
- ✓ Industrial networking

Building and security:
- ✓ Alarm systems
- ✓ Video intercom
- ✓ HVAC

Low power:
- ✓ Glucose meters
- ✓ Power meters
- ✓ Battery operated application

Appliances:
- Motor drive
- ✓ Application control

Consumer:
- ✓ PC peripherals, gaming
- ✓ Digital camera, GPS platforms

Now, there are other applications like appliances, motor drive, application control, industrial application controllers, and there are a lot of consumer devices that have an architecture and are built on the cortex and core like PC peripherals, gaming, digital camera as platforms. So basically you can find architecture based devices and cortex based devices everywhere around you. You just need to look and try to find the word arm on that microcontroller or controller inside your device. These are sound applications, but you are not limited to these applications. You can do anything with these amazing calls.

NUCLEO DEVELOPMENT BOARDS

Now, let's talk about the Nuclear Development Board. Now we are talking about the sport as an example. You can get any other ball, but you should look for these main features in any development board that you are going to use in your arm and arm architecture, development and learning curve or let's say learning journey. So. This is basically the board. And it's based on the ah cortex and for architecture, it has one megabyte flash memory, 128 Kalabi, Esraa data memory, and it has a clock frequency that can go up to 80 megahertz. It's basically built on the same 32 all four hundred seventy six MCO. Now let's talk about the main features and this Dysport. There are still 32 nucleo 64 boards that provide an affordable and flexible way for users to try out new concepts and build prototypes by choosing from the various combinations of microcontrollers. For the compatible boards. The exterior lessened significantly, reduced power consumption and run are on the three connected with support and the ESTIE more for headers allowing the easy expansion of the functionality of the SDM 32 Norcliffe Open development platform with a wide choice of specialized shields. Now, the I'm 32 nucleo 64 board does not require any separate probe as it integrates that stealing Bogar program, that's the 32 nucleo 64 baud comes with the SDM 32 comprehensive free software libraries and examples available with the stem cells to Appu MCU package. Now let's talk about the common features of these boards. They are based on a STEM 32 microcontroller. They have one user led. Shared with Arduino, they have one user and push buttons at thirty two point seven kilohertz, crystal oscillator and basically the bolt connectors, they have Arduino only three expansion, Connector estimates for expansion, pennyfeather for full access to all ASTM, 32 input output pins. They also have flexible power supply options.

The NUCLEO-L476RG Development Board

- STM32L476 MCU:
  - Based on the **ARM Cortex M-4 Architecture**.
  - 1 MB Flash memory, 128 Kb SRAM Data Memory.
  - Clock frequency: up to 80 MHz.

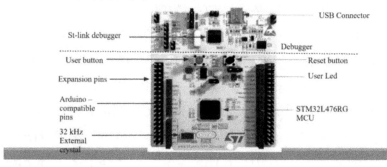

They have on board stealing the Bogar programa. They have comprehensive free software, libraries and examples. They support a wide range and choices of integrated development environments. Now, when it comes to that border specific features. It has twenty four megahertz, which is E and it has a lot of connectors. Now, let's take a look at the board itself here, as you can see in this picture. Here we have the stealing Dibakar. And basically, this is it. Now we have the crystal that we mentioned, and you can find that there 32 kilohertz external crystal is here. These are the Arduino compatible pens, and as you can see, they have the same pinout as Arduino, about three fold, five on the ground within a zero to a five and other pens as well. And this is a very great feature. You can place any Arduino shield right here. They have expansion pins right here and right here, which gives you a lot of options to connect different devices. And the upper corner is the debugger corner. Here we have a USB connector that you can use to connect your PC and then you can run the SD cube software or any development environment. Now, it doesn't require a programmer as it has a direct USB connection to the PC, which is a very nice feature. Now, this is the main brain and our board is the ASTM 32, ORL 476, R.G., MCO or microcontroller. This is the. Button, and this is a user pattern that you can use for debugging and development and as you can see, it has everything you need to get started with the system and even have a user led. As you can see, this is the load and you can easily. Control that led using your code and let's say make a code that whenever someone presses this user button, it will turn on this user outlet and this will be one of the first calls that we are going to create anyway. This is one of the boards that we recommend. Some people might find it a little bit expensive. So we'll show you another option that you can consider when it comes to something to develop. But that's it for this lesson. If you have any questions about this board, you can look it up or you can ask in the Q&A board and I'll be more than happy to help you. Now, the main features here is that it's Arduino compatible. It can be connected directly to your PC for development and debugging. It has two buttons. One led that you can use. It has expansion pins. And it's basically an all in one development board that you can use to get started in the architecture world.

STM32 DEVELOPMENT BOARD

Today, we'll talk about our less expensive and easier to purchase bold and stamp 32 development board that contains the ASTM 32 F. 103 C, 80 C. This is the bar, it's a very small board, but it has a lot of options that you can use to start developing your AR applications. This different board contains the 32 Cortex M3 CPU chip from the SDM 32 series, which is cheaper and more powerful than the well-known Arduino such as the atMega328 chips. It is even possible to simply program these chips via the well known Arduino ID. This board works on three point three volt tazz, a 64 Cailloux Bitel flash memory, 20 kilobyte of Islam and a clock frequency of eight to 72 megahertz. Now let's talk about it in more detail. It's more support power and it has a two world bit. One microsecond analog digital converters, up to 16 channels, all support the army and has up to 80 fast and put out reports and some of the modules now all support the Bagnold and has seven times and up to nine communication interfaces. Now it comes in different versions. But for this version that we have here, as you can see, it's a very small version and it has a reset button. Now. Now, when it comes to the pin out, let's take a quick look at these pants up here on the left side, you can see that we have to ground pants, this one and this one. We also have a three point three. Volpone watches this pen and we have the reset button pen right here. Then we start with the input output pens. Now, B1 means part B one. Bauby one. This is 11 one or 10 sorry, and one so here we have one, 10 and 11 for or B, we also have zero. Now, starting from here, you can see that we have pens that are related to a and usually these pens support ADC on this side. Starting from B 11 now. B1 right here has all support for ADC, ADC and this one now, as you can see, a one, a two, three, four, five, a six and a seven. We also have a zero. We have C 15. C, 14. C, 13. These are sea pens, and here we have Obinze zero, one, two, three, four, five, six and seven. These pants can be used as input output pens and some of them support analog digital converters. Now, as you can see at the end, here, we have another band that's called V, B or V battery, and this band can help with connecting our microcontroller to a battery. So this is basically a battery pin. Now, from the left here, you can find the USP or micro USB port and we will show it to you. And a practical lesson here. We have to jump to control the boat. Here we have the main microcontroller and here we have a reset button. Right here you can see PC 13, which is basically a read that you can use for debugging. And this is the power left. Now, this is the main Cristel that our microcontroller uses, and here you can see that we have a debug interface, it has four pins and each of these pins has its own. Connection and when it comes to these bones connection, you can see that we have a three point three Volkman right here. And at the end, we have a ground ban, so this will be connected to ground and this will be connected to a three month revolt. Now, these two pens are used for debugging. The first one is called the. I all input output and this is the clock, Ben. So this is for input output data and this is 4:00 and they are labeled as the clock and S.W., the input output, these are used for debugging.

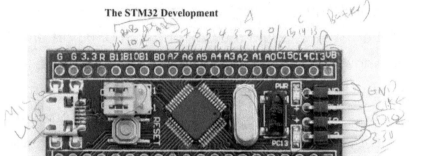

We also have a pin here that we already mentioned. It's that it has been right here. You can connect it to a button to reset the microcontroller during the debugging phase. And these are basically the main pins that you need to care about. Now, let's move on and cover the rest of these pins. Don't understand that most of these bands are input output bands. So from here, you can see that we have 12, so this will be. What, Pippin's 12, 13, 14 and 15. Here we have brought a band up to this point. Here we have eight, nine, 10, 11, 12 and 15. And here we have more people and three, four, five, six, seven, eight and nine. And here we have the five Volpone. Here we are around. And here we have another three point three Volkman. So this is basically the board has a lot of pens. It's a very small board, so you need these pens to a pen here and connect it to an. Our breadboard is sorry, so that you can easily interact with it using the debugging software. This is the world that we will use as we go with this course, and we will teach you how to write a code, how to control the built and learned, how to connect different peripherals, and how you can reset the bug in your code easily.

INTRODUCTION TO ARM WORLD

We're going to talk about R or a R now is the leading technology provider of processor IP offering the widest range of Brussels to address that performance power and cost requirements of every device. Octopus and NPR use include cortex, a cortex and cortex are and other cortex that are available on their website, AHAM stands for Advanced or ACORN Risc Machine. ResCare stands for Reduced Instruction Set Computer, which is basically a technology that was adopted, almost founded in 1990. They provide CPU chips, physical compilers, system on chip and infrastructure, and they donate about 75 percent of the market. Now, R is also written in small letters that were previously on a column for advanced risc machines and originally ACORN Less Machine. It's a family of reduced instructions, said computers, and it's basically used for computer processors. It's configured for various environments. That's why there is more than one cortex.

And we will talk about that and details in a few minutes. Now they provide a system on chips, which is OSSE and an armatures system on modules. There have been several generations of arm design. The original arm one used a 32 bit internal structure but had a twenty six bit address space.

About ARM

- ARM = Advanced/Acorn RISC Machine

- Founded in 1990

There are a lot of details to this, but what you need to understand at this point is that R stands for Advanced Risc Machine and it's basically a company that provides C.P.U design for different purposes. Now, our main customers in the market are on this list, as you can see, until Samsung and we have Broadcom, AMD, Apple, Qualcomm, Lenovo. All of these are customers and they use arm design. So if you have an iPhone to have a computer that uses an Intel CPU, you might find our logo on that CPU and we will discuss different boards that use our architecture. But it's good to know that arm is available everywhere. Now, regarding ARM processors, there is more than one processor technology provided by ARM.

ARM Processors

- Cortex-A (Application)
  High-end embedded OS, MMU. Ex: Smart Phone

- Cortex-R(Real-time)
  Ex: BlueRay players, Hard Disk Drive controllers...

- Cortex-M(Microcontroller)
  Embedded System, replace 8051

And what we are going to discuss here is only three of them, the main three. And we will deal with Cortex only because it's the microcontroller based cortex. Now, the first one is Cortex, an estancia for applications. It's high end embedded or us Ammu like smartphones, like Apple devices and some of the Samsung smartphones while cortex are, which stands for real time, specifically for Blu-ray players, hard disk drive controls and other things that require real time response. Such devices cannot afford a little bit of delay when displaying a movie using the Blu-ray players, for instance. So the cortex is for this purpose. There is also Cortex, which stands for microcontroller and it's mainly used for embedded systems and it plays the 1851, which was an intel processor that is very famous in line with the system work. Now. Again. You might have heard of Mediatheque CPUs or Processors that are used in most of the Chinese forms, they are all based on the arm or arm cortex. A7 again stands for application seven is the CPU architecture generation and it can go up to one point three gigahertz. Now, we need more information about this. You can visit the site on dot com slash index dot p HP. Now let's take a quick look at the arm cortex. AmCham again. M stands for a microcontroller. This is an embedded system Chip. And in this image, you can see a few things that you must be familiar with. Here we have Abbas.

ARM Cortex-M Chip

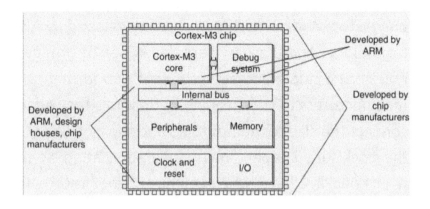

Abbas is basically around that. The chip used to transfer information from one location to another and vice versa. Here we have the core of our CPU. This is the whole thing. Here is the cortex M3 chip. Now it has memory. It has her Theron's, it has KI Andrew said it has input and out all of these. Are connected to the internal boss and to cortex and three core, now three three here is the generation and each of these generations has its own specifications. So what you need to understand from the previous slide is that a sensible application R stands for real time. M stands for microcontroller and whenever you see a device and smartphone, you must know that this is used. This is our phone that has a browser that uses Cortex A because Cortex is the most powerful one and its main use for smartphones. Understaffed, whenever you see an embedded system based device, you must know that it's using cortex. Going back here, Cortex and Core are connected with a debug system and these two that the bug system and cortex M3 core are developed by ARM technology. And these two are developed by arm design houses and chip manufacturers, so it's up to chip manufacturers to choose what peripherals they need to connect the size of their outputs and the clock and reset the clock speed depending on their application. So the whole package here, when you buy it from a store, it will be developed by chip manufacturers, not by our I'm usually licensed chip manufacturers to use their design of the core of the system and other stuff inside that chip. And they just sell them the right to develop the final product using their technology. Now it's up to the chip manufacturer to create the final design using the ARM company original design. But they all work together to give you a very fast device using arm based processors. Now, for instance, Oncolytics XM. On version seven architecture, there is no cash and no Alemu now MMO stands for memory management units, so that ship doesn't have a memory management unit. It supports the instruction and interrupts automatically. Save Restore state. They have fixed memory maps and the thumb to process core blasts, high code density. These are some of the main features for arm cortex processors. Now other cortex and versions might have different specifications. So you need to choose the one that works with your application. Now, for instance, as you can see here, we're still talking about armed conflicts and here you can see this green box. It has the Cortex, M0, M1, and you can see how many instructions here. And you can also recognize that it's not a lot of instructions. So this procedure cannot be used with embedded applications. That has a lot of instructions.

ARM Cortex-M

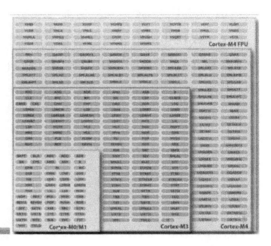

And you need to do a lot of things inside them, connect a lot of sensors and do a lot of mathematical operations. Now, after that, there's Cortex M3. It's that blue area here and it has like four times the number of instructions. And then Cortex and Ford have even more instructions and Cortex and for FPO and as you can see, it has more instructions. So as you go up with the number, this is a very important formation. As you go up with the number after the letter, you will find that the processor is more powerful and it has more instructional support and it can address more memory. Now, that's it for that introduction to our world. I hope that now you understand that ARM is not the company that manufactures the chips. They sell the manufacturing rights to other companies like Apple and Orvil, Intel, etc.. ARM stands for Advanced Risc Machine and race stands for reduced instruction, said Machine. Now a stand for application called M Stand for Microcontroller Cortex R stands for real time. Now, if you do understand all of these things, you can move on with the cause. Otherwise you have to play this video again to understand things and try to write them down. If this is your first time with ARM technology.

INTRODUCTION TO ARM CORTEX

What is called Cortex is our next generation arm processor, it consists of classic CPU and system peripherals. There are three series of this type. There are areas and we are dimensioned these three times and we discuss them and details. So the series is for complex applications and operating systems. Also, this is for real time systems and this is optimized for the cost of our sensitive systems. There are like 15 performance levels and zero is the lowest. Now, let's talk about the cortex, CPU and salvage specifications. First, you need to know that the 32 bit risk, 32 bit risk is basically the CPU structure or what you can define.

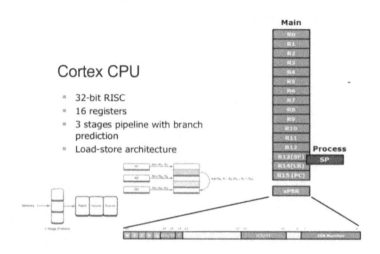

The CPU with risk is reduced instruction, set computer architecture. It has 16 registers. It has three stages of pipeline with branch protection. And it supports Loadstar architecture. Now, as you can see in this image, these are the registers from R zero up to 12, then 13, 14, 15. And this one is 16. Now, we mentioned that this is a 32 bit architecture C.P.U. So you can easily recognize that we should have 16 or 32 bit sorrys. If you look here, you can find zero. This is the X PSR register and we won't go into details now here. It starts with zero. And the last bit right here is 31. So from zero to 31, these are 32 bits. Which is basically why this is called a 32 bit press cluster or risk architecture. Again, these are the 16. Each one is 32 bit in width and it has. At three stages, pipeline with branch prediction, when we talk about the three stages, you can easily see here that we have the code and execute for each of the instructions. This is basically the internal structure of our cortex CPU. And the one that we are talking about here is a 32 bit risc architecture CPU. The cortex M3, for example, has two modes of operation and two levels. The operation Morns Threat Mode and Tandler Munsterman, without the processor, is running a normal program or running an exception handler like an interrupt handler or system exception handler. That privilege levels provide a mechanism for safeguarding more access to critical regions, as well as providing a basic security model. When the processor is running a main program and threat mode, it can be either in a privileged state or a user state. But exception handlers can only be in a privileged state when the processor exits. Racette is in threat mode with privileged access right in the state program, has access to all normal ranges and can use all supported instructions. Software and a privileged access level can switch the program into the user access level using that control register. Now, when an exception takes place, the professor will always switch back to the privileged state and return to the previous state when exiting the exception handler. It is a program that cannot change back to the privileged state by writing to the control register, it has to go through an exception handler that programs that control register to switch the process or back into the privileged access level. This happens when returning to treatment.

CPU Operating Modes

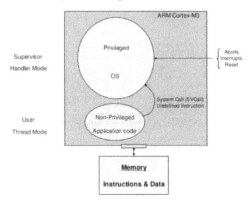

Now, as you can see in this figure, these are the available operating modes and privilege levels. Now, if we take a quick look at this schematic, you can see here that we have supervisor handler mode and we have the use of red mode here. We have the privilege, which is the US. And here we have that unprivileged application called. Now, system calls or as we call, undefined instruction from the privileged. And here you can see them, a movie that has instruction and data while it's connecting with the CPU and it's towards. So, again, the cortex M3 has two months of operation and two previous levels, the operation models are called red mode, which is this one and handler mode, which is this one. This determines whether the person is running a normal program or running an exception handler like a sports interrupter or it. We are talking about the cortex M3 here, but you can use the same, let's say, definition with any other CPU that follows arm design. Now, let's talk about some instruction sets. Some technology was introduced in the arm 1156 call, it was announced around 2003, and it extends the limited 16 bit instruction set of thumb with additional 32 bit instruction to give the instruction set more breadth, thus producing a variable length instruction set. A stated aim for some two was to achieve chord density, similar to some with performance similar to the other instruction set on 32 bit memory. Thump to extend their thumb instruction set with battlefield manipulation also of our staple branches and conditional execution. At the same time, there are instructions that were extended to maintain equivalent functionality in both instruction sets and a new unified assembly language, or you et al support a generation of either thumb or arm instruction from the same source code. So what you need to know here is that the thumb to instruction set is basically a 32 bit performance with 16 bit chord density it needs for Nantasket c. And this image, as you can see here, explains everything. For the context, M3, you can see that we originally had some instructions that were 16 bit. Some, too, as we already mentioned. Came to extend their limited 16 bit instruction set of thumb, which is this one with additional 32 bit instructions to give that instruction set more breadth. This is the only thing that you need to understand from this whole thumb to instruction setting thing. And we will talk about that in more detail in the coming lessons.

Thumb-2 Instruction Set

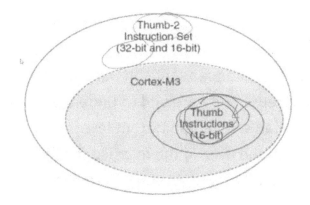

Now let's talk about the emolument. As you can see, this is the map in our arm cortex, CPU's, as you can see here, we have the court, which is the lowest area, and this area is basically dedicated for our court and it can go up to half a gigabyte. Then we have the static ram that can also go up to half a gigabyte. We have a specific place in memory for peripherals that can also go up to half gigabyte. And we have the external ram that can go up to one gigabyte and the external device memory that can go up to one gigabyte. Then we have private peripheral, both internal and private parts, external plus the vendor specific. Now the vendor specific is up to the vendor. They can place anything they want in this area of memory. But this is the main structure for them or memorium. Absolutely. In the cortex CPUs now.

WHAT IS CMSIS

This is basically a cortex microcontroller software interface standard. And this is what s.M s I. S stands for. This is a vendor independent software layer that will export and reuse software and to understand it more. Details you can see here, different layers that we must go through from the user to the microcontroller. Now, let's start with the first layer. As you can see here, we have the application code, that application code is basically the user layer. And if you look here, this is the name of the player, so the application code will go through real time kernel and middleware components and some of its components might go all the way through to the peripheral register and interrupt vector definition and to the device perform functions. And some application codes might communicate directly with the code peripheral functions. After that, you can see that we have our team or us, which is basically the second layer. This is basically the real time kernel and the middleware components that stand between the application code and the system as s layer. Now, the layer that we care about here and the main topic and this last one is this layer, the third one seamless is it's basically a layer that has core profile functions, middleware access functions, device peripheral functions and prefers to just start and interrupt. Victor Definition. All of these are inside this layer. And that's why this is a very good standard that makes it easy to communicate and reuse software and code. This layer communicates directly with the MCU, the MCU layer has the C.P.U, which is mainly the brain of any ambient system system or embedded software system, and we have this tech, which is the art to the Oscar time. We have the NVC, which is basically untested.

CMSIS Structure

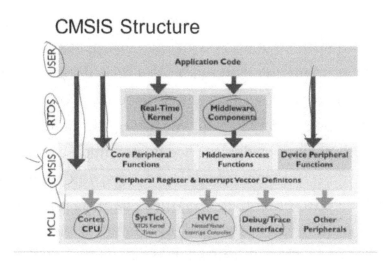

Victor interrupt controller and the backtrace interface and other peripherals. So this layer helps the application code from the user to communicate with the MCU or the cortex CPU layer. And we are using this to make it easy for us to develop and write codes for the MCU. Now, again, this is basically a vendor independent software layer. This will ease porting and reusing of software and these two points are very important and you must keep them in your mind. Now, the file structure when it comes to this layer is as it starts with ASTM 32, the text, which is the main file, it goes to two files, the Lacau and the System file. Now, the court file has the study and the text file. Now, this is the file structure. And here we are explaining each of these branches, the court system three, the text is basically the cortex M3 global decorrelation file. The court system 3.0 is the cortex M3 three, global definition. And we have the court system three that X these are truly independent files and we have the device text to be included in application software depending on the type of device that you are using. We also have a system devised to take. This is the device specific declaration. We have the system device to see. It's basically a device specific definition and all of these files. Help initiate our layer. Now, you might think, do I need to remember all of these names and all of these guys know, most likely the development environment that we are going to use will handle everything. You just need to create a new project and most of these files and definitions will be created for you.

ARM CORTEX M4 ARCHITECTURE

First, you need to know that this microcontroller supports Harvard architecture. It has a 32 bit Hafford based architecture, has some 32 instruction sets, which can go from 16 to 32 bit instructions. It has caused jester's level of zero two or 12 as these are just cells that are general purpose. It also has a stack pointer, a PC program, counter L.P link register and an AP is a programmed status register. It also supports unified memory space up to four gigabytes onto a bus interface based on the arm a b a defines the communication between the microcontroller modules through the on chip buses. That is a HP, the high performance bus connecting the Antioco elements for less delay. And there is the A P B Perforin pass. It has a low bandwidth connection with the paraphilias. Also had MVC controller interrupts and exceptions.

- 32-bits Harvard based architecture
- Thumb-32 instruction set (16/32 bits instructions)
- Core registers: R0...R12 general purpose, SP stack pointer, PC program counter, LP link register, APSR program status register.
- Unified memory space 4GB
- On-chip bus interfaces: Based on the ARM AMBA (defines the communication between the microcontroller modules through the on-chip buses)AHB (High-performance bus) connecting the MCU core elements.
  - APB (Peripheral bus). Low-bandwidth connection with the peripherals.
- NVIC controller: Interruptions and exceptions management with priority handling
- Systick timer (24-bit decrement timer).
- Optimized for low power consumption. Various sleep modes available.

Management, with priority handling it had a system stack timer which is 24 bit different timer, and it has optimized or optimization for low power consumption. Various sleep modes are available and we already mentioned that. Now, if you take a quick look at this picture, you can see an example of the arm architecture design, the system here, which is basically. This bus. But here. The blue line. Connect the core elements like the professor up here. And flash memory, but from Islam, which is basically different types of memories for different purposes, also connect that the bug interface, whereas that peripheral Buzz Lightyear. The one that we just mentioned, which stands for A, P, B, deals with the connection of all MCU patrols, both of these past channels are interconnected by a bridge managed by a master slave mechanism following the arm specifications. And you can see the bass bridge right here. So they are connected using this bus bridge, but each of them connects different elements.

ARM Cortex M-4 Architecture

- Example of the ARM Architecture design. The system bus (AHB) connects the core elements (processor, memories, debug interface) whereas the peripheral bus (APB) deals with the connection of all MCU peripherals.

- Both bus channels are interconnected by a bridge managed by a Master-Slave mechanism following the ARM AMBA specification.

And as you can see, this is the system controller. This is the processor. This is the bug interface flash memory, both from RAM, which are things that are very important and cannot afford any delay in communicating with these parts, but it can't afford delay in communicating with these peripherals. That's why they are connected to a secondary pass called Peripheral Bus, which is connected to that timer RTC and output pens and digital converters and digital converters that can pass. And the A.C., your art S.P.I communication protocols, plus the Ethernet controller if available. So what you need to know is that inside the arm cortex and for architecture, we have two buses. One for the main processor, the second is for the professionals.

ARM CORTEX M4 MEMORY MAP

We mentioned that the other space can go up to four gigabytes, which is sometimes for some projects itself, very little space and for other projects, it's a very big space. Now, this is the memory we're starting from here. You can see that we have a code area that can go up to five hundred megabytes or have a gigabyte. This is an area that is used mainly for a program called it can also use for exception, vector table. And as you can see here, this is the starting atlas now. Above it, you can see the Osram that has the very same size and small use for that memory, which is basically a static ram. And Islam stands for static. Now, above that, we have that person's memory that is mainly used for films like Oscar, CSPI and other communication protocols.

- Address space: 4GB, little/big endian

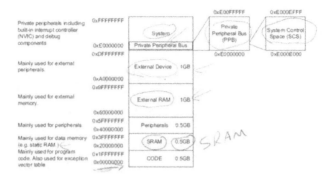

We also have a one gigabyte external RAM that can be addressed. It can go up to one gigabyte. It's mainly used for external memory, for things that are not very important, like storing data. Now we have an external device memory that can also go up to one gigabyte that is mainly used for external peripherals. Above that, we have that system memory, which is basically a private peripheral, including build and interact controller, and we icey and debug components. Now it has an area called Private Peripherals Bus that has a private bus B and the system controls space, which is S c c. So this is how that four gigabyte can be separated among different things inside the arm cortex and for memory map. Now somehow it has four gigabytes, some one gigabyte, depending on the type of ball that you are using and the normal specifications that this board has. Again, it can add up to four gigabytes, which is a very nice feature that you can use.

DOWNLOAD AND INSTALL STM32CUBEMX IDE

I will teach you how to download and install the system 32 Cube Development Environment. This development environment is provided for free online. All you need to do is write ASTM, 32 years old. Idea or development environment now this is the first result, ASTM 32 cube idea, which stands for Integrated Development Environment. This is an advanced CC + + development platform with powerful configuration cogeneration called compilation. And the bug features for Stampfel to Roubaud now. It goes right through to that download page and in here you can find all the features and different versions. Now, if you have Linux, you can download. The software. As you can see, we have a deep down, we have a giant Kleenex installer and we have a knockwurst version, we have R.P.M. version for Linux and we have the Windows installer since I have Windows operating system. I'm going to download the Windows installer. And as you can see, the latest version is one point, six point one. Now, if you are interested in another version, you can click here and select a different version from the list we usually recommend downloading.

Read more ⌄

Get Software

Part Number	General Description	Software Version	Download	Previous versions
STM32CubeIDE-DEB	STM32CubeIDE Debian Linux Installer	1.8.1	Get Software	Select version
STM32CubeIDE-Lnx	STM32CubeIDE Generic Linux Installer	1.8.1	Get Software	Select version
STM32CubeIDE-Mac	STM32CubeIDE macOS Installer	1.8.1	Get Software	Select version
STM32CubeIDE-RPM	STM32CubeIDE RPM Linux Installer	1.8.1	Get Software	Select version
STM32CubeIDE-Win	STM32CubeIDE Windows installer	1.8.1	Get Software	Select version

More from the product line

The latest version has bug fixes and a lot of features. So click get the software. This is the license agreement. You have to accept it so that you can download the software for free. Click accept. Now they will take you to the software page. Now the main goal from this page is to take your name, your last name, your email address to send you their announcement, their new software releases and other stuff. So you can write your first name, second name and your e-mail address, then click. I have read and understood the cells. Now, if you want to be informed about future updates of the software, you can take this. Once you're done, click, download and. It will direct you to that download. Page, as you can see, your frustration has been successfully submitted, now, usually you receive an email that you need to validate your email address. Now, once you receive the email, you can go. You'll find a start your software download email and it will have the download. Simply click download now and you need to use the same browser. Now, your download will start and you will get a file. This is the file that you will get, usually it's a zip file, so you have to extract it using any of the software that you have and if you don't have one, you can download one.

It's a free software tool and the files are simply extracted. Once you are done, you will get this folder and this is the file DoubleClick. And your installation process will start Zarkasih now simply hit next, I agree, next, give them selected. And as you can see, this will solve the cigar dealing driver. And this was said to be a stealing drive.

Now it's extracting and installing the files click install. Now, it shouldn't take long, as you can see, it will keep extracting files. And installing them on your PC. And just to make sure that, you know, what is this that we are installing, it's basically ASTM 32 cube idea, which is an all in one multi or as development tool that is a part of the system 32 cube software ecosystem. It's basically an advanced CC + + development platform with Peiffer configuration cogeneration code compilation and the features for ASTM, 32 microcontrollers and microprocessors. It is based on the eclipse framework and see toolchain for the development.

It allows integration of hundreds of existing plugins that complete the features of the eclipse idea. As the ambassador to Cuba, Ali integrated the configuration and project creation functionalities from ASTM 30 to cube mix to offer all in one tool experience and save installation and development. Now, after the selection of an empty stadium, 32 MCO or MPU or configured microcontroller or microprocessor, or from the selection of a board or the selection of an example, the project and this idea will be created and initialized and it will help you in generating your code. Now, at any time during the development, those are returned to the initialization and configuration of peripherals and middleware and regenerate the initialization code with no impact on the user code, what what's really great about this software is that it combines the code generation code compilation and the bug feature for the Stamp 32, which is what we are learning in this course. I'm sure that you will start using this platform, develop a lot of your future projects. So what you need to do is to follow our steps to get this software up and running on your machine. As you can see, the extra cash extraction and installation process is about to finish. Now we are done simply at the end. Now you can download software from the start menu or from your desktop icons. Simply Head Start attempted to cube Ivy. This is a. We'll take a few seconds to load it now as you select either through as workspace now as the answer to Cube idea, use the workspace directory to store its preferences and development artifacts. Now, you need to store these things in a place that you can go back to if anything wrong happened. So we don't recommend using your main drive and a Windows operating system to solve the workspace simply had Prouse.

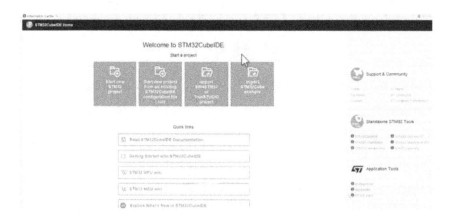

And go to another directory like the E and call it. Justin. Or expect. Simply selected select folder. That's it. Now you can take this option. Use this as default or the default and ask again so that you don't get this message every time you open up the software. Now, at lunch. Starting the answer to Cube Ivy. That's it. Now you have the idea you can start a new project that allows access. Now click, yes, you can start Neuralstem 332 project here or you can start a new project from an existing email TOKYOPOP X if you already have a previous version, or you can import your projects or import examples all the time to talk to you. Now, this is the support and community links. This is the Sandrone, a STEM 32 tools. These are the application tools and these are some quick links for the SDM 32 AMPE Wiki and MCO wiki, plus the documentation and the getting started manual.

DOWNLOAD AND INSTALL ARDUINO IDE

Which is an Arduino ID. First, you must go and search for Arduino I.D. using Google or Bing. The first is Windows, you see, which is the official Arduino website. You can either use Darwin Web editor without installing software or you can download the Arduino ID now, depending on your operating system, you must choose one of these Windows, Mac or Linux for my case, its Windows installer. Now it's asking you to donate or you can just download. Click on Save. And you have to wait about three minutes for the download to finish. Now let's see the Arduino website. It offers. A lot of products. As you can see here.

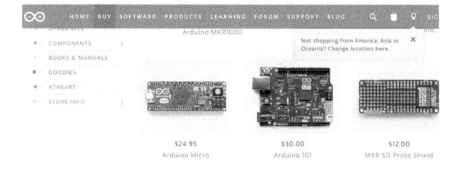

You can share any of these items from the official
website. These items include Arduino boards. Green kids
and a lot of other interesting stuff. Now let's see the
other kids category. As you can see, this kid, um, this is all
about kids. It has a very. A very interesting collection. You
can also buy Arduino boards or windshields. Let's look at
boards and modules and see how much each of these
boards might cost you. This is the official place to buy
Arduino boards.

Sort By   FEATURED   ▼

ARDUINO
ALL PRODUCTS
MKR FAMILY
BOARDS & MODULES
SHIELDS
KITS
ACCESSORIES
RETIRED

CURRENTLY SOLD OUT

$39.90
Kit Workshop - Basic level, without Board

$39.40
Rural Hack Kit

$94.99
mBot robot V1.1-Blue (Bluetooth Version)

You need to make sure that you are not buying from places that offer a fake ALGUIEN on boards or boards that are not manufactured, bought by the original company. The export of arms to. Can also check the learning section for tutorials, reference and things on new things to learn. As you can see here, the boards, the entry level has only Leonardo and starter kit. No, no mini micro. The enhanced feature has the Amiga, the Internet of Things has other. As, yes, I'm shielding the proposals for making, let's say, a smartwatch, the printing section for making a 3D printer. Let's see the Ormeau. And the mega. This is, uh. Arduino material one zero one, a symbol 3D printer. As you can see. Looks. Mines will cost you around 700 hundred dollars. You can also see the arguin on board. It'll cost you 25, 24 dollars. Twenty five dollars. Aldwin, onum. As you can see, this is the original stuff. Now, in order to move your borders or not, you can flip it if it's a symbol in USA or Germany, then it's original.

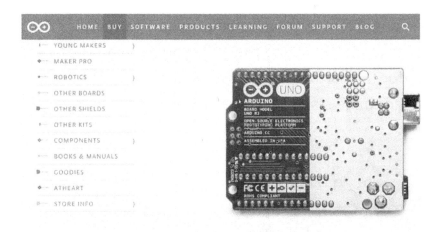

The ones that are assembled in China are not created by the official Arduino company. It's created by Arduino associates. And it must cost less about ten to twelve dollars or debauches such bolds. They are not there and don't have the same quality as the ones manufactured in us. OK, now let's see the Arduino finished downloading, let's run a download Arduino has already installed, so you have to understand the one that you have. OK, let me see. You have to close instances, we all know that you have opened, then uninstalled. The previous version. As you can see, it's removing the files. If you already have an

Arduino installed in your computer, you need to update it with the latest version if you already have the largest version, and then please skip this lesson, click on next install, as you can see, the installation or start. It won't take long. You can check out our resources section, discoursed to download the code and the material to get links for the hardware material. OK, and I had to close then go to the start menu. Go to the Eleazar, then choose Alino.

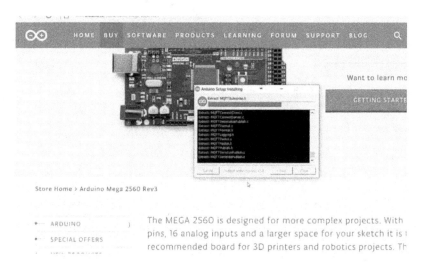

This is our original idea. Now, to make a quick overview, this is the button that you must click to verify that your code is written correctly. This one is used to verify and upload Dakota Arduino. These are for orbit and save this to create a new file. As you can see, when you create a new file, you have two main methods: the setup and through the setup for your setup code. The loop is for your code that will run repeatedly. And the fine is common sense, Skitch is used to upload, verify the code or add new libraries. The tools as used to choose the ball, shoot the ball, get the ball, inform, choose the programmer Bernard Bootloader, which is an advanced topic, and Arduino open the Syrian monitor or Syrian Blätter fix the encoding of the code or the IT help is where you can find things. You are looking for its answers. Now you can check example's basic digital analog communication controls and sort of display. Uh, let's see that we want a basic example for blinking led. As you can see, this is a blinking example. It's very simple, straightforward. It's commented so that you can understand what's happening and what's going on. So that's why Arduino is very good. Popular because it would provide amazing support.

CONFIGURE ARDUINO IDE TO PROGRAM STM32 BOARDS

Now after downloading and the price of Arduino Idy, you need to go to your Web browser and some derived stem cells to Arduino then, right? GitHub. Go to the second result, Roger, click on it and you will get this one, as you can see, GitHub, polar slash Ilda a.T.M 32, right. Click and click, download zip file. Now, click, start, download, and it won't take long.

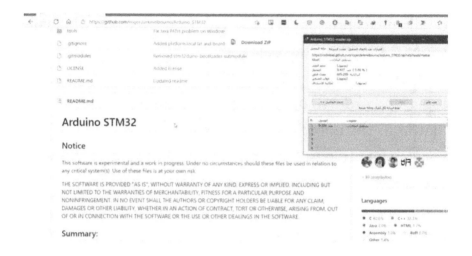

Now, this is a software or this software is experimental and I work in progress, so you might face some bugs, but it's a very great software or let's say library that would allow you to program as TMZ to board using your Arduino I.D., which is something you are familiar with. Now, we will wait until the download is finished and we will start. Adding these files to our Arduino folder. Now, as we are waiting for the download to finish, you need to go to your Arduino. And this is the original idea.

We already explained how to download and install this idea. Now you need to go to the tools. And here you'll find that in the board we don't have Arduino Astrium 32, and to give this board, we need to go to the boards manager and here we need to install Arduino on some boards. You will find that third result here. Sorry, arduino some boards and these are boards included in this package like the Altuna do, and it supports the 32 bit arm cortex and three. So to add the support, simply install. Now, the installation process will begin with about a 60 megabyte file, so it will download this file and once you download this file, install it, it will add Arduino or sorry, 32 bit arm cortex, M3 support. And this is something we need before we copy the files from our GitHub library to Arduino folders.

```
#include <ESP8266WiFi.h>

int port = 8888;
WiFiServer server

const char *ssid
const char *passw

int count=0;

void setup() {
```

Now, as you can see, done and stalled, and if you have this word, then everything is slightly closed and hit the close button again. Now for hitting the close button, you need to know exactly where is this Arduino software version located? Now go here, right Arduino right click. Open fire location. And from here again, right, click on the Arduino and you need to trace the software now click properties. As you can see, this is the installation directory simply copy that installation directory placed here based. And remove cardinal. That's it now we are inside the Arduino software folder. Let's close this now. We finished downloading the library files from GitHub, so we need to extract them, so go here and let's see, this is the library Abdinur attempted to master, simply extracted. Here it is and here is this. This is Arduino 32 m. Now copy that file or that folder and based it inside the hardware folder, inside Arduino. So you need to make sure that you are programmed files, Arduino hardware and then paste the Arduino ASTM 32 folder right here. That's it. Now, it will take about half a minute to copy all the files. Now, as you can see, this folder has also an ever folder for the microcontroller. And now we are adding support for the Stamp 32 microcontroller. Great, now, once you are done, simply go right, are doing again. OpenNet. Let's minimize these. And you'll wait. For all the idea to load, to show you how you can select are doing or serving SDM 32 ball from the original idea and this is the easiest way to program, is to attach strategy to balls using the original idea, because most people already are already familiar with the Arduino idea. Now, from here, you can go create new sketch. Go to the tools and go to the board. Now, once you go to the board, you will see that now we have ASTM Albino's to search to master drivers and we have ASTM albinos to master tools and we have stem cells to EF1 boards attempted before boards. Now, from this list, you can select the board that you have and usually it will be one of these Jaric boards, but we will talk about that in the practical section.

For now, let's say that you have selected this board. You can go back, make sure that this policy answers to F 103 three series is selected and you can select the variant from here. Now, some Borshoff 64 Caillaux flash memory, and some other boards have 128. And you can select the upload method using ASTM 32 Luigino Bootloader. If you have a boatload on your board or using Syria connection, stealing or using black magic Propp, you can even select the CPU speed. The normal is 72 megahertz and that's it. The last thing that you select is the port.

STM32 ARM NAMING

This annual Lars von Trier, going to talk about ASTM 32 is named and we are going to cover the pin out and that just registers inside this microcontroller MCU. Now, let's talk about the naming structure. Usually you will find the CPO name, starting with ASTM 32 like here. Now, in this area, you can see that we have ASTM 32 and this is usually the first thing that you will find when you look at the CPU. Now, the second thing that you will look at is that letter F, and this is basically a product type and it's usually followed by, let's say, a number. And this number has an indication now, for example, let's write or let's try to figure out the naming mechanism for this MCU. Let's say that we have a microcontroller called SDM. 32. G. And 431 Arby, now this is a very long time. It starts with a 32, which is the MCU and is the product type.

STM32 Arm Naming

STM 32 G 431RB

Field	Description	Some Valid Values
STM32	Product Family	Arm⁵ based 32-bit microcontroller
F	Product Type	
4xx	Device subfamily	407: STM32F4xx
L4		446: STM32F4xx.
		L4: STM32L4xx,
		and so on.
P	Pin count	K = 32 pins
		R = 64 pins
		J = 72 pins
		M = 81 pins
		O = 80 pins
		V = 100 pins
		Q = 132 pins
		Z = 144 pins
FFF	Flash Memory size	B = 128 KB
		C = 256 KB
		E = 512 KB
		G = 1 MB
?	Packaging	LQFP
6		temperature

Now, it's usually followed by three numbers: L for execs like that, L for execs or simply you will find four execs. Now in this case, we have four execs and this four is followed by thirty one. Now, this is basically the sub category for the device and it's followed by the PIN count. So here we have an. This is a pin count. And to know how many pins you have. You can refer to the stable or mean that this is a 64 bin MCO. This is just from the letter after these three numbers. OK, now what about that letter B is basically the memory or flash memory size B here refers to one hundred twenty eight kilobytes. So this is how you can easily read the name of your ASTM 32. Now, sometimes the name is followed by. Two more. Digits. And these are the packaging types. The first one is the packaging type and the second one is the temperature. But usually this is the whole name again, starting with a stamp 32, then the product type, which is G, then that device subfamily, which is 451, and the PIN count, which is the first letter, the Fleshman sides, which is the second letter. So whenever you see an attempt to mce, you try to read the number, try to figure out how many bins this MCU has and what is the flash memory size from the MCU. And just to make sure that you understand things, I will give you one.

STM32 PINOUT

Now, as you can see, this is the El Que F.P. 64. It costs 64 pence. And it's easy to recognize these pens. And I will teach you how to do that. Now, to get started, you need to understand a few things. The first thing is that whenever you see PE. Then it stands for pot, whenever you see A, B, C, D after this, B, this is the port. No, or they are. So here we have P.c which means PERTZYE. Seven, here we have let's say he to Holtby. Five support people, five and so on, you can use this with any other pen. Now, we also have video depen on power. We have an Aspen Aspen ground. We have a battery, Ben, if you want to connect a battery. And we have that asset bin where you can connect a button to reset the microcontroller. We also have less to talk about as we do the same power pins. Another video depen, and this is basically the whole thing. Now we have both zero pins and this pin is used for controlling the bolt mechanism inside our MCU. And you can check others. Configurations, as you can see here, we have an Elche package with 100 bins, and as you can see, it starts with one inch with 100. And it has bought me the battery little pens, and it has all the different spins.

STM32F4xx LQFP 100 pinout

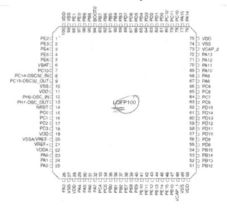

And here we have versus with the power pins, we have bought Bayport, we bought the Bauby again, Potsie bought A and here we have bought he bought the pork pie and bought and this is the board. So it has more support, it has more pins and it's suitable if you have a lot of input outputs that you need to interface and connect. Now this is a partial listing of several others. Map for a 32 EF four hundred forty six. As you can see, the name is AHP one. And you already mentioned this. Now this is the address and this is that peripherals connected to that address here we have general-purpose input output. It means that general-purpose input output pins. This is the port. Which is edgy if the CBA and I so it has all of these sports, these two addresses are reserved for the device manufacturer. These are time events. This one is for S.P.I. See no communication. These are for artificial convergence. These are for you as an Artisphere communication. Diamonds and. As you move on, you'll see more modules, sorry, like the square, see you, Artie. I square as a spy and RTC four o'clock. These are timers and here we have a digital converter. Here we can see our communication protocol and everything has its own boundary address. And each of these peripherals is connected through a bus to our main MCU. Now, some of the larger purpose and put up registers that are important and you need to know how to configure them will be explained in the next lesson. But that's it for this lesson. We explained the pin out and how to know what each of these can do and how to recognize the pins so that you can easily connect them.

SOME OF THE GPIO REGISTERS IN STM32

What you are going to talk about, some of the major purposes and put out registers and ASTM 32 effort on. So here we have the address of each of these resistors. And here we have the name. Here we have a description on at right now, Armin's read women's rights. So read, write, register. Now, the address is basically the address of each of these registers. And Mummery, the name is the name that you are going to use inside your code when you are using C language. Now, whenever you see X in the name, it means that. A, B, C, sometimes D, E, F, G, H, and I, and this refers to the part that this register is being used for. So if you are using the first register, it's called general and but output, not X, let's say a 440 modder. Now, modern means the Portmore Register M or the mood register. So it's the general purpose, input output, export mode or direction of the staff, and it controls the direction of this board, whether it's input or output. Now, that general-purpose input output, X or type, is a register, it's basically an output type register. So it configures that type of the output that we want to send. So if you are using a board as an output, you can configure the output. Taib, using this register. Now, some of the pens can be used for high speed data transmission or for high speed, let's say, encoder and pod treating and to control the output speed there is Algester for that is called general-purpose input output X or speed or means output speed register. So this is used to control the output speed and we have a pull up and pull down resistors inside our MCU. Now some of these bands support that, others not. So to control this, whether you want this resistor to be operable down, you need to use this. It's called PUE. These are Kolob down-registers. Now there is a port and an Algester, which is an IDR input data register to control the inserted data or the data that you used your MCU to read. There is also an output data register that will control the data that you send out using your MCU. And there is a bit set Racette register that you can use to set or set any of the input outcroppings or any of the registers, all the bits inside them, inside your microcontroller.

Some of the GPIO Registers in STM32F4xx Arm

Address (Offset)	Name	Description	Type
0x00	GPIOx_MODER	GPIOx Port Mode(Direction) Register	R/W
0x04	GPIOx_OTYPER	Output Type Register	R/W
0x08	GPIOx_OSPEEDR	Output Speed Register	R/W
0x0C	GPIOx_PUDR	Pull-Up / Down Register	R/W
0x10	GPIOx_IDR	Port Input Data Register	R/W
0x14	GPIOx_ODR	Port Output Data Register	R/W
0x18	GPIOx_BSRR	Bit Set / Reset Register	R/W
Where x=A, B, C, D, E, for ports			

So these are the main adjusters and you will probably see some of them when you call this the M 32 microcontroller. So let's move on. This is the data and direction registers and a simplified view of an input output. Now, as you can see here, we have a pen and so on, let's say, a pen. Five ports. S.. This is basically one bin. Now, this is a bit of the IRS, the IRS effluent pack, you will see that the IRS means data input register. Now. This is one of the registers now and out between now and now, this in case you are using this pen as an output, it will send the output signal to this pen.

The Data and Direction Registers and a Simplified View of an I/O pin

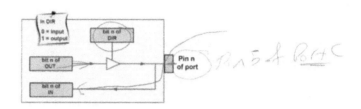

Now, if you are reading a signal, it will give the signal and receive it stored inside that bit number of any means, the input register of this bolt, which is in this case, Portsea. So each of these pens has an output and an input bet that you can use to either send or receive data to this specific pen now. And they are for data input registers zero means and put. And one means output. This is basically a quick schematic just to show you how each of these pens and our MCU is structured and how it is used to receive or send data.

CONTROL REGISTERS IN STM32

New show is going to take a quick example for using and coding general purpose input output patterns. Now GPI stands for real purpose input output, which is basically a digital and put out. Now, input is basically when a program can mind if input signal is one or zero output. When a program can set output one or zero, you can use this to interface with external devices or on board peripherals like switches and buttons and input or LEDs and speakers in case of output. You already know this information and.

Basic Concepts

GPIO = General-purpose input and output (digital)
Input: program can determine if input signal is a 1 or a 0
Output: program can set output to 1 or 0

Can use this to interface with external devices or on board peripherals
Input: switch, button......
Output: LEDs, speaker......

In this image, you can see that we have some 30 to 40 x MQ AFP 100 package pinout, and from this image you can see that we have. Here we have 110. And we have bought them. Up to the party, so we have A, B, C, D, E. And these are one, two, three, four, five, Holtze. In this 100 pound package, not all pawprints are available, so sometimes you might find that PIN five bought A is not available or B has two options that are not available. So you have to work what? With what works and what's available, and in this case, the available pens are written in this pen so you can know what works and what does not. Now, that depends on package pin count. So here we have 100 pins.

STM32F40x LQFP100 pinout

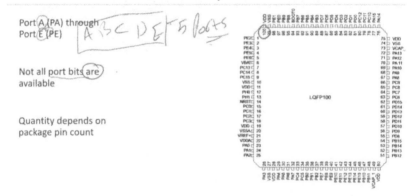

Port A (PA) through
Port E (PE)

Not all port bits are
available

Quantity depends on
package pin count

There are other packages that have 64, 32. So depending on your application, you have to choose the right package. Now, the general purpose input output board bit circuitry inside the MCU. As you can see, we have configuration, we have data and we have the looking. Now, we want to explain this, but I will explain the main points or sections inside here. We have read here we have right here. We have a read right now. As you can see, the output data register, which is all the area, is basically read right. Register a bit. Set research to register is allowed to register now the input data register by the hour is already registered. So each of these passes can be read, written or read. And right now, here we have, as you can see, an output alternative function input. And this is going to be on Chipperfield. Now, here we have an output controller and we have driver and output driver. All of this is inside the MCU for Michael Controller. Now, what I need you to understand is that there are specific registers and we already explained them in a previous lesson. Some of them might be read, others. Right. And that is read right, as you can see here. And you have to know exactly the abbreviation for each of these registers because we are going to use this in the coding section. Now, regarding the configuration, you can go figure that direction than you x the mode, the speed.

GPIO Port Bit Circuitry in MCU

Configuration
- Direction
- MUX
- Modes
- Speed

Data
- Output (different ways to access it)
- Input
- Analogue

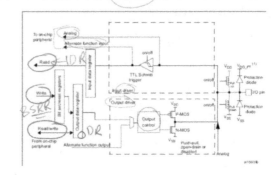

And regarding the data, you can output data or get input data or deal with analog data. Using these different points, you can even lock the data or use a locking mechanism to lock the CPU and a certain. Now. That control register I want to explain again, but we will do a quick overview, each of our purpose and what our support has for 32 bit registers. The first one is the mode part, which is basically the mode control system that defines the report as input output analog or any other mode. Now there is also another GISTER called output type register. This is basically a register that controls the output type, whether it's Push-Pull or open train. There is also the speed control register or output speed register that controls the speed of this thought. And there is the APU PDR, which is the pull up all down register that enables all up or down, depending on your specific application and the hardware that is connected to our port. Now there are 232 data registers. The first one is called. Ideal, the second Odera, and we already mentioned this, this one is basically the input data register and this is the output data register. Now, a 32 bit citrus register is also available, and as you can see, this is what this register stands for, bid citruses to register. Now, this is the blocking register. It's L.K. are stands for log register.

Control Registers

Each general-purpose I/O port has
- four 32-bit configuration registers (
  - GPIOx_MODER (input, output, AF, analog)
  - GPIOx_OTYPER (output type: push-pull or open drain)
  - GPIOx_OSPEEDR(speed)
  - GPIOx_PUPDR(pull-up/pull-down)   *input*   *output*
- two 32-bit data registers(GPIOx_IDR and GPIOx_ODR)
- a 32-bit set/reset register (GPIOx_BSRR)   *BSRR*
- a 32-bit locking register (GPIOx_LCKR)
- two 32-bit alternate function selection register (GPIOx_AFRH and GPIOx_AFRL)
One set of control registers (10 in total) per port

Each bit in a control register corresponds to a port bit

All registers have to be accessed as 32-bit word

And there are two 32 bit alternative functions. Election register called a alternative function register and other one alternative function register. L stands for law, which stands for High. Now, one set of control registers, which is basically 10 in total. So if you did a few halftime, you can count this. Here we have. Four. And this one is we have two here and we have one here, one here and two so two to four and to six. So four plus six equals 10 resistors. So each port has ten control registers. And this is why programming Estienne, 32 is not as easy as programming a bit. Microcontrollers requires a little bit more, uh, let's say, advanced experience. And we are going to help you with that. Now, each bit in a controlled register corresponds to a board bit. Depending on how many spins inside this port, we have a 32 bit register and not all of them are used to that to control just now, all adjusters have to be accessed as 32 bit work. Again, we already mentioned that, but sometimes some of the port pins are not available. So we might sometimes use 18 bit from these 32 bits. But when we are accessing them, we have to deal with this as a 32 bit register. Now. What I need to understand at this point is that we have ten general purpose registers or let's say 10 control registers that are associated with each of the polls that are available inside our MCU. Now. This is the major purpose, input output configuration registers, each bit can be configured differently. Racette clears board with direction to zero. So whenever you initiate a set action, it will put zero in that inside that bed that you are trying to set. Now, output Maude's includes push all or open train plus all up or down. The output data from output data register, which is all the are all professionals using alternate function output. Now, the input state is basically floating up or down or analog. Then put that to that input to just start, which is ideal or perfect a lot, it's, say, alternative function. And so whenever there is input data. It will be stored inside this register whenever there is output, data will be stored inside this register, which is either the R or the alternative function output register that we already mentioned in the previous slide. Same thing for that. Now, output has these modes, input has these machines, and that is it adds zero to the specific bet and each bit can be configured differently according to your application. Now, as you can see in this image, the right side here, we have the model register. Here we have the type register here. We have the speed register here. We have the pull up all down register here. We have the input output configuration. Now, as you can see, this is the first mode. And as you can see, each of these bits is configured differently according to the application. And here we have the speed mode.

GPIO Configuration registers

Each bit can be configured differently

Reset clears port bit direction to 0

Output modes: push-pull or open drain + pull-up/down

Output data from output data register (GPIOx_ODR) or peripheral (alternate function output)

Input states: floating, pull-up/down, analog

Input data to input data register (GPIOx_IDR) or peripheral (alternate function input)

MODER(i) [1:0]	OTYPER(i)	OSPEEDR(i) [B:A]	PUPDR(i) [1:0]		I/O configuration	
01	0	SPEED [B:A]	0	0	GP output	PP
	0		0	1	GP output	PP + PU
	0		1	0	GP output	PP + PD
	0		1	1	Reserved	
	1		0	0	GP output	OD
	1		0	1	GP output	OD + PU
	1		1	0	GP output	OD + PD
	1		1	1	Reserved (GP output OD)	
10	0	SPEED [B:A]	0	0	AF	PP
	0		0	1	AF	PP + PU
	0		1	0	AF	PP + PD
	0		1	1	Reserved	
	1		0	0	AF	OD
	1		0	1	AF	OD + PU
	1		1	0	AF	OD + PD
	1		1	1	Reserved	
00	x	x x	0	0	Input	Floating
	x	x x	0	1	Input	PU
	x	x x	1	0	Input	PD
	x	x x	1	1	Reserved (input floating)	
11	x	x x	0	0	Input/output	Analog
	x	x x	0	1		
	x	x x	1	0	Reserved	
	x	x x	1	1		

1. GP = general purpose, PP = push-pull, PU = pull-up, PD = pull-down, OD = open-drain, AF = alternate function.

Here we have the pull up, pull down resistor and you can choose how to configure each of these. Now, if you did see peepee you have in the data sheet or g.p, gibi stands for the purpose. Yippy stands for Push-Pull P you. This stands for All Up while PDA stands for pulldown or D stands for open train. F stands for alternative function. Now, this is how easy it is to read a data sheet and to assign values depending on the application. Now, alternate functions. This is basically the F register in F mode, F or L and F our edge, which stands for alternative function, just law, alternative function of just some high needs to be configured to be driven by specific perfetto. So you have to configure it yourself. It can be seen as a select signal to the Immunex, which is the multiplex. Now event out is not mapped to the following input output panels, which are Pkwy 13, 14, 15 zero one and P eight.

This is the event out and we are going to talk about it in the advanced tutorial about ASTM 32. Now, what I need to understand is that we have the ultimate function selection register. And this is basically what I just thought of that must be configured to be driven by specific peripherals that we are connecting to our system. And you can see in this image that this is the F area and this is the F r edge. And here. It starts with F zero. And ends with A15 here also starts with F zero and ends with F 15, now that this is the event out that is not mapped onto this fence. Now, these are the pens and you have to connect them accordingly. So let's say that you want to connect all using the S.P.I protocol. You can use these Tobins. What about, let's say. Connecting our t protocol on a device that works using your CRT, you can use these Tobins. So depending on the powerful and the communication protocol and what you need to do exactly, you can use this alternate function selection register.

PRACTICAL WALKTHROUGH SHOWING THE FAMOUS STM32 DEVELOPMENT BOARD

I'm going to take you in a quick walkthrough to see this development board. Now, this is A.T.M 32 Development Board, and you can buy it online. Let's talk about the package. This is the first Jumba. And that's Sobolev. This is everything that you have inside. This is the part we'll talk about in a minute. These are the opinions that you need to shoulder right here in your board and you can buy a version that has all of this been sold or already, as you can see here. These are the pens. And these pens provide easy access so that you can place the board on a breadboard and connect the front wires to the front end and what happens? So you have all of these pens, you can solve them yourself or have someone sell all these expenses for you. Now, these two are called jumpers. As you can see, these two pieces are used to choose different ones for this board. Now, the first moment is the, let's say, execution moment. When you have a code loaded in this board, you can place these two jumpers here. And the second one, I decided, OK, sorry. Let's make sure that we are connecting them correctly. In this direction, and there's no actual talk about that or and the practical outcome of this course, but let's move on now.

These are the jumpers. This is the recipient. See, this is the CPO. Now, let's talk about the components and this wall. This is something from up here. This is the USB interface and this is the board select jumpers. This is the reset button, as you can see. And this is the MCU or main microcontroller. And you can see let me show you a stamp, 32 F. As you can see, it's written by their one hundred three C eight six. This is the version of this MCU. Now here we have an oscillator and under it right here we have crystal. So this is the main oscillator. And this is our crystal, as you can see, thirty two point seven key. Now, here we have the first lead, which is PC 13, which is the PIN number and will use this. And according this is a built in just like an Arduino, and you can easily use it to test your. Here we have the power indicator led and. Now, as you can see, we still have this, which is basically that the bug interface and underneath these pens, you can read the words written. I don't know if I can show you these words from this angle anyway. This is the three point three wall. The last one is on the ground. Ben, this is the clock. Ben and down beside it is that data input output. So these are the four pens.

Now, if you flip the board, you can see that we have a voltage regulator here. Now, this is a three point three volt regulator. It will take five volts and convert it to a three month revolt to bar the board. Another thing that we need to mention here is that these numbers, when you are in the execute sequence, you must keep them that way. If you want to load a new code to your board, you have to move this number one up here. To this location, it will leave the first pin on the wall connected across these two bands and then press the reset button on your upload process. Now, how to program it will explain that and a lesson. But this is everything you need to know about the sport when it comes to the main component. Now, regarding the pins from the left here, we have two ground pins, one three one three. Well, then let me use a pin to show you what I'm talking about. So ground three revolt. Ben, this is the reset button. Ben B, which is an input output. Ben B, 11 ten one zero. Basically, this is part B and here we have a seven, six, five, four, three, two, one and zero for A and here we have Potsie, 13, 14, 15. And here we have Ben that you can use to connect an external battery. Here we have both P again, then ballsed A. Then Bauby. And here we have five open grounds and three point three Volpone. Now, if you want to turn or to power your ball, you must connect five volts on the ground.

Or if you have a three month revolt source, then you can connect it and connect to ground. Ben right here to turn the ball on. But we usually use the five Volpone underground beam and the voltage regulator will take care of the regulation on voltage and it will turn the five on to three one three volt. That's it. This is everything you need to know about that. STAMPFEL To Achieve Development Board. The sport can be used to start implementing your architecture coding and we will use it for the practical lessons of this course. We'll explain how to program it using our idea and how to program it using Cube and X.

SOLDERING STM32 PINS

Show you how you can easily sell the pens to your stambaugh. Now, if you have a.T.M board and the bins are not soldered correctly or not soldered at all, you can simply shoulder the expense by following my steps. Now, let's start by connecting the pen header to our board the right way. First, you need to place them like that. These are the first set of twins. These are the second set of twins, after placing them like that, you need to place them all on solid ground. So. Now, let's also dispense with it. Well, this.

Now, start by holding those pens in the corner. This one is misplaced. Now, after shouldering the Four Corners, as you can see here, these are the Four Corners now the pain header is placed and we can proceed with shouldering the rest of these pins. So I have soldered this, this, this and this. Now, I will proceed with these pins, so let's do it. That's it for the smoldering process and as you can see, all the expense is now soldered correctly and we haven't done anything that you can see their plastic yellow that protects the pens is still there. And we have zero space between. The board underpins something here. And all of these pens are now connected and you can start using the board. Now, usually. We connect this board to that.

CONNECTING STM32 TO PC VIA FTDI

We are going to load our first code to the ESM 32 development board and discord will be transferred using this FTT or this USPI to the AL. Programmer. And as you can see, it's basically you ask people grammar and have these out three month revolts. These are the background and the five Volpone. So it's fairly simple to connect this to our board. Now, what you need to understand is that we are not going to use that bug interface to load the code.

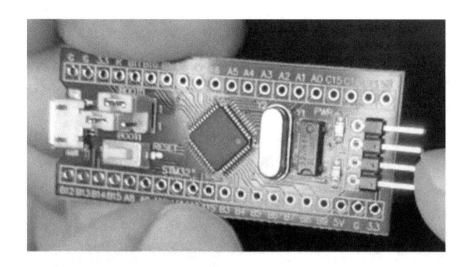

Some people mistake this as the seal interface for uploading codes. But what we are going to do is the following. We will connect this. USPI or after the eye programer to our ball, and we will provide more to the sport using this program. We will also connect the text and our expense, the second and third pens to our A nine and eight and pens on the F.T. or this Deum 32. So let's start connecting these elements. Now what we need to connect. We don't want to connect that three point three volt. We need to connect the five volts, ben. And the groundball, so this is the five Volkmann, and at this point we are doing that, we have a victim of five Volkman, which is the spin. Now, you should surrender the pens here and connect them to a red ball. This will be more convenient, but I'm just showing you how the connection should be made. Then I was told that these wires or these pens to them. Bill Hader, now, the next bend that you need to connect is. The ground then, so that Blackburne is the ground pin.

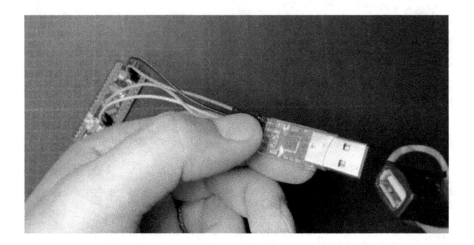

Connected to you. So now we have a five ulpan underground connection. Now we need to connect the ah expen. Which is the white pin to the airline. And the expen to a 10 years. That's it, and this is basically the connection and the next step will be. Connect this USB connector to your computer now.

INTRO TO STM32CUBEMX

We will cover the main features of this tool, which is you to configure and generate code, plus the compiling and debugging process. It also helps you estimate the power consumption for and third, to the family of microcontrollers. So. As you can see, while this lesson is specifically about the ASTM, 32 zero and basically what applies on zero can be applied on any other attempted to make it controller, but we are specifying a specific family here so that we can study everything about it and you can take the knowledge and apply it to any other microcontroller. Now.

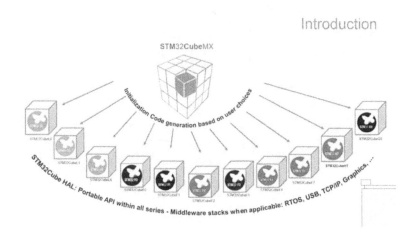

As the answer to Cuba is a common platform to the hall is the answer to family, so you shouldn't worry about having to learn a new software for each new SDM 32 version that you are trying to use now. The answer to Cuba's application helps developers using stem cells to microcontrollers through a user interface that guides the initial configuration of a firmware project, it provides the means to configure pain assignments, the clock, three integrated peripherals and simulate the power consumption of the resulting project. It uses a large library of data from the storm surge to microcontroller portfolio, and the application is intended to ease the initial phase of development by helping developers select the best product with regards to features and power. So the main application benefits here is that it helps choose the correct MCU for a given purpose. Simulation provides an advantage and design fails. It boosts development speed. With a head start, you can choose an ideal MCU and simply configure Pinault clocks and oscillators, Burwell's lobar modes and middleware.

- Choose ideal MCU and simply configure
  - Pinouts
  - Clocks and oscillators
  - Peripherals
  - Low-power modes
  - Middleware

Application benefits

Helps choose the correct MCU for a given purpose

Now. Some of the key features. The user interface is built around a natural workflow of choosing a suitable MCU, selecting the required peripherals and assigning pen configurations about consumption, calculator AIDS and designing an efficient system. Finally, the project initialization code can be generated and potentially regenerated while keeping the user code intact. So some of the key features of this user interface is that you can control their peripherals and middleware parameters. There is a power consumption calculator that you can use to know exactly how much power your MCU will require. There is the cogeneration feature, which makes it possible to generate code while keeping user code intact. And that is the option of command line and batch operation that is expandable, let's say libraries and you can plug-ins. There is an MCO selector, you can filter by family package peripherals or Moses's.

- Peripheral and middleware parameters

- Power consumption calculator

- Code generation
    - Possible to re-generate code while keeping user code intact.

- Option of command-line and batch operation

- Expandable by plugins

- MCU selector
    - Filter by family, package, peripherals or memory sizes.
    - Search for similar product.

- Pinout configuration
    - Choose peripherals to use and assign GPIO and alternate functions to pins.

- Configure NVIC and DMA

- Clock tree initialization
    - Choose oscillator and set PLL and clock dividers.

You can search for similar products. There is also a panel out configuration where you choose peripherals to use and assign general-purpose input output and alternate function to Penns. You can also configure advice and diamé from the user interface. You can also use the clock three initialization, which allows you to choose Oscillator Ansett PLL and clock dividers. Now let's talk about the fact that there are a lot of ideas that you can use to deal with your Steam 32. There is the stem cells Tsukuba mix that helps you generate the code. There are a lot of partners' ideas that let you compile and debug your code. That is, that stands to you, that will help you monitor your

MCU. And there are a lot of free ideas that you can use. And this is a list of them. The Estienne 32 has a lot of support.

STM32CUBEMX MCU SELECTOR

Now let's start a new project and see the MCU Selector now after your open system, 32 Ubaidi Click Start, New Estimator Tool Project. As you can see, this is what we call the MCO Selecter window, and it only comes up after selecting the new project option. Now the user knows which MCU to use and it can be found quickly. If not, the available products can be filtered based on the specific requirements. Now, if you want to, uh, let's say, filter the results, you can start filtering them by package, which has been counted the Ramsey's and minimal requirements, embedded reference number and type of interfaces, color and frequency. Plus the price. Now. Once you are here and in this window, you can write to your partner and I know for sure that I have SDM 32 F, 103 C.

And the one that I have is C six now. Some people have C eight once you select the path number four, which allows you to show up here and you can see a lot of information about it. As you can see, it's like a mini datasheet that shows you the features, how many pins that flash memory, the low power requirements and the configurations plus the peripheral that it supports. And this is the price, as you can see, in USD. So about two dollars and this is the package. It has forty eight pins, calcu of pre packaged. And here you can see also the information is like a summary of the package, the flash that arm outboards frequency and the reference type. You can also go to the blog diagram, you can see the death sheet if you click, and you want to open up on your page with the data sheet for this specific MCO. So the support provided is very great. This is the data sheet, as you can see. You can see everything there is. It's about a hundred seventeen pages. Let's close this. Now, there are other documents and sources that you can use. And there is a place to buy if you click the by button, it will redirect you to the store for a stamp, 32 products. Now, if you don't know the name of your MCU or that number, you can search using the code. And the one that we have checked has three core cortex and you can remove it and start filtering them by the court. Let's say that we want M0 then here we have different areas, F series and you can choose the line. You can choose. The package. As you can see, that two point four to eight, four 100 bins and now we have two that matches our specifications. And if you have other specifications, you can specify a preference here. As you can see, everything is filtered. And now we have two that match what we have specified here. Now, another option other than the MCU and CPU selector is the board selector. Now, the board selector is basically a way to select a board instead of selecting NMC or UNPEEL. There are a lot of M 32 based boards and as you can see, this is a very large list of them. Now, you can go here and check the boards or the P. L bought the SD evaluation boards, a lot of options again, and here you can select the vendor, you can select the time for Discovery Kit Evaluation Board, and the boards will basically be filtered according to your suffocations here. You can choose the system that you want to use.

And some people come here to buy a board. So when they find this board, they usually. Click here and select the buy button to buy it from Estienne Electronics Shop. Again, this is another option that is also an example selecter. As you can see, you can see the board endurance, the productize or project type sorry, the middle where peripherals and other stuff. Let's say that you want a digital converter example. As you can see, these are the boards that support this example. There is also a cross selector and basically you can select your MCU using the backlists on the left here and you can filter by the vendor to say that you want a microchip board and from here you can select. But it needs an Internet connection, and basically the one that I use is the MCU. I always like to use their part number and the CPU or MCU number. And again, my MCU is SDM 32 103 C. This is everything you need to know about The Selecter, let's write SDM 32. One hundred f one hundred three. A. Let's check everything here, ASTM Thursday too. The. And basically, you have a lot of things. Are selected little things, ASTM, 32 F, 103 C. And click once now this is the ball that we have here, the next lesson we are going to talk about the pin out and pin assignment inside SDM 32 Cube.

PINOUT CONFIGURATION

Now, after selecting our MCO from the list, the next step is configuring or selecting the peripherals to be used and where applicable, assigned bands to their inputs and outputs. Now click next after selection of MPU. And here, you need to write a project name, let's call it first. Project, we will see, and we need it to be executable and we will use stem cells for you. Now you can click next to keep configuring things, but I will click finish and I will leave everything as it is. Look, yes, do you want to open this perspective now? Now it will start initializing device configuration. And it will download some files that are required for this specific MCU and in here you can see the print out for our MCU.

Now, independent general-purpose input output can also be configured, signals are assigned to default bins, but they can be transferred to alternate locations which are displayed by these bins. Now. The tool or the software that we are using here automatically takes into account most bonds between the peripherals and software components it manages. So you don't have to worry about anything. Now, once that is done, we can reconfigure the pins according to our connection or depending on what we want each of these bands to perform or do. But you need to understand that the software has automatic signal remapping, and that is management of dependencies between peripherals and or middleware like USPI and other connections. Now, before moving forward, I need to tell you that we are using BlueBell's import and export based on the absolute that I have chosen here, ASTM 32. I will zoom in so that you can see Astrium 32 F 103 discs. And this is the number. Now, this is a state controller at a world that is based on the 103 C six are like the one that we have.

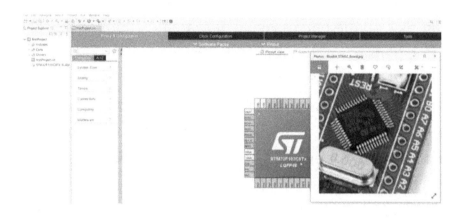

These are the Ramble fans, and they are identical to this MCO. You can see that here we have. Le Pen's Bauby was seven. And here we have 40, here we have bought a hair, we have bought about P and here we have four P and bought Abram's. All of these are our purpose input output bins that have not been assigned yet. Now we know for sure that the bluebell. Board has allowed it. And it's connected to PC 13, so you need to go to the PC 13 bin, and from this list you can choose what is the function that you need this pen to perform. And in our case, we need it to control Aland. So it will be our purpose, input output, pen output. Now, there are other options like input. There is RTC out, RC tamper or set status, analog pen event out input output, external interop 13 or any other function. Now once you configure tenpin, you will see that the cloud is now green. So let's talk about things you can click on the pen to view alternate functions so any of these pens has alternate functions and you can click on it to see the list of these functions. Now, if you saw an orange pen, this means that the peripheral or peripheral is not enabled, only the pen is assigned. Now, when the peripheral is not enabled, this is a case for that. And we will talk about it now if you see up here. This means that the MCU has to freeze the signal placement using the pen icon. So the signal is now purpose, input, output, output. That's why there is a pen here. Now, sometimes you need to connect up well and it's not available. How can you check that? You can go to the Times and if there is a red circle beside the official name or profile name, you will know that this is used and you cannot use it. These are all the pitfalls that you can use with this MCU and as you can see, you have diamonds, you have RTC, you have ADC, which is our digital converter. You have different connectivity protocols. I CCSVI your safety and the can bus plus the USB pass. And there is the CRC computing function and that is middleware like the three hours to optimize. So these are the main functions that you can assign. As more pins are reserved for the ultimate functions, the choice of remaining configuration for other peripherals decreases. The limitations are indicated by icon changes and other peripheral nodes. Left click on the pen to display its alternate functions as well, as we already mentioned. Now, if you want to right click on the pen, you can name it with a new name or select the pen assignment so you can introduce our label. And here you can see. Glemp. As you can see, this is by right clicking that pin, you can do signal and spinning, you can pin stacking or you can change the name simply by right clicking that pin. If a pin out is selected without a particular peripheral enabled or if there is any other problem with a pin out, the pin turns orange and green instead of green. And in this case, you have to check the wording or the error message. Now, another thing that we need to talk about before moving forward is that there are three or four different possible states for peripheral modes. There is the damned state in which the mood is not available because it requires another mode to be set. Place the mouse pointer over the demo to see the reason. And it may require a disabled clock source or have other peripheral dependencies. That is, they, Lord. This mode is available with limitations, so it shows you that the pain is available with limitations because some options are blocked by conflicts. For example, the US Army may not be configured to Synchronoss mode because all selectable pins are taken.

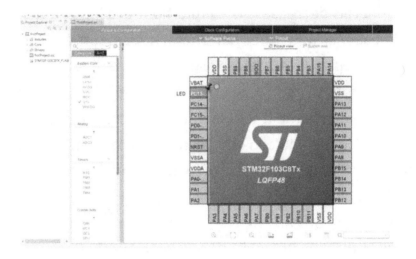

And there is that mode where a signal is required for this mode cannot be made. To that point out, this Milkha, for example, if a crucial signal has all its alternate pins used by other peripherals. Now signals can be set or moved directly from the pin out view, which is basically this view, you can click on the PIN to display the list of possible signals and select one. This works for general purpose and output pins, which have no peripherals assigned. It's not necessary to manually sit all unused pens until there is a semi automated step that does this. So you can ignore unused pens, since the coal generator can set them to power, saving and allocating. That's it for the spin out configuration, and we will talk about the peripherals and middleware configuration and the next lesson.

PERIPHERALS AND MIDDLEWARE CONFIGURATION

Go talk about peripherals and middleware configuration.
Now, the global view of yours, peripherals and
middleware is basically the place where you can configure
if you switch up in our view and system view, you can see
that we have a lower section and we have a peripheral
section. Here you can see the system called we have the
army, we have general-purpose output, we have in Visi,
which is a nested Victor interlock controller, we have the
RCC, which is that asset and control we have assist. This
preference is correctly configured and you can generate
code using the current values. Now, this green sign, there
are three or four types of signs. If you saw this green sign,
it means that this is If you saw a blast sign, it means that
it's not configured.

If you saw a yellow rectangle, it means that there is an unblocking problem and you can generate the code. If you also have an X, which is added X, it means that there is an error. Now, this is where you quickly switch between the Pinart view and system view. This means that the configuration is valid because we have a green check. Now you can click to configure the Diamé and you can add, but we won't do this right now and there is also the general purpose, input, output and configuration. And if you have configured something, as you can see, the peripheral is currently configured. And if you haven't configured anything, if you haven't added any pins, you might see the rectangular yellow swirling. But it's not an error. And the cold may be generated now here. Is everything we have and once you click on any of these, you can easily configure now we talk about the configuration separated on the configuration tab of the main window provides an overview of all the configurable hardware and software components that ASTM set to Cube Amex can help set up. Each button with access to configuration option is displayed with a small icon indicating that configuration is state, the default state is not configured like you can click on a button for a perfect appleford or middleware displays its configuration just like what we did here. Now, even configured correctly, further modifications are possible. As you can see, this

one is configured correctly, but we still can do more
configurations. Warning signs provide notifications about
incorrect configurations and peripherals will not work if
code is generated in this state.

Now, critical errors are represented by added X and the
configuration must be modified to continue to add more
peripherals and components. You can return to the pin
out tab and here and you can click and add or simply click
on any of these peripherals that are available. And here
we have the middle word. Now, after reading them, you
can configure them from their system view or from this
menu. Now, we don't have any middleware right here,
but each middleware software component has options
that are different. But they are all presented in a similar

fashion, giving you easy access to initialization options and providing informative descriptions. So whenever you add a new middleware. You will see that it has options just like any other configuration tab, and you can configure everything.

FIRST STM32 CODE

We're going to start with the first steps to configure ASTM 32 to blink alerts. Now, this is a blanket example and it's a very basic example just to learn how to deal with inputs and outputs. Now, the first step that you need to do is. Select the oscillator, you need to go to that low configuration and here to the right, we have a line here. To the right you can see that we have the internals of the MCU, the internal clock, that preschooler and other configurations to the left. Right here we have input frequency and we have to select one of these two to be as an external oscillator. So to verify what this line is, the external configuration and to the right is the internal oscillator configuration. Now, what we are going to do here is go back to the pinata configuration and in here select our sushi. Now, RACC stands for Racette and Cloke Counter. Now, once you click that, you will see a window. And this is basically the high speed and low speed clock configuration you need to select a crystal ceramic resonator. Now, why did we choose crystal ceramic resonators? It's because we have the I'm 32 blue pill board. And on this board we have a crystal ceramic resonator that runs at eight megahertz now.

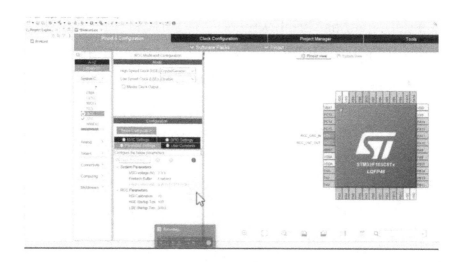

Now, what you need to do is go back to that clock configuration and from here you need to select AC. Here now in this area, we have the high speed clock, which can run up to 72 megahertz, which is the maximum speed to change this number to 72 megahertz. And presenter, you will see that there's an error. No, you need to go back to the pin out on configuration and in here you need to make sure that PC 13 and which is participant 13 is Mark General-Purpose Input Output Output per. Once you are done, you can move on and go to the left and right here, select this, and from here you need to select the debugger that you wish to use. Now, depending on your specifications, if you have a specific debugger, you can check it out from this tag. But we will use serial wire, as we have on USPI or Acidify cards that we will use to connect our PC to SDM 32 Global Board. Once you select the debugger as serial, why do you see that two more pins turn green? Now. These are the two pens that will be used for the serial debugger. After doing this step, you need to click on the device configuration tool. That will help you generate them. And this tool is this gear icon, as you can see, device, configuration, tool called Generation Click once and click. Yes. Now, as you can see. The device configuration tool is updating the code and here is your second. Now, if you weren't here, you will see that you have a lot of files. You have binaries you have and include the core files. The man that either the men, the sea and the main part of that you are going to work with is the core source men to see file. Now, inside this file, we want to explain the whole coding structure. You need to go directly and make sure that you are inside the main method, inside that you will find one loop while one this is an infinite loop in which you are going to write our code. Now, just to make sure that you understand what's happening here, we are going to use the library. To start using this library, you need to do the following. Now click here and start writing by Tal. And GP eyehole. Then if you want to see the list of things that are available, you can press controlled blast space and you'll see a list of the functions available in this library.

The function that we will need is that toggle pin function. It takes two parameters. The first one is the general purpose input output letter. And in this case, it will be Port C. And the other. Configuration input is the general purpose and output pen, and in our case, it will be. The. And 30, so we have jumpers and put out what, Ben, 13 and this means PC 13. Now the second step is adding a delay. Highlight how underscore control plus space and delay. By 500 means five hundred milliseconds, and this is how easy it is. That toggle function will toggle the state of this pen, which is Pkwy 13, participant 13. So the built-in lid will turn on. Now, the second time this loop runs, it will toggle the state from on to off and so on. This is a 500 millisecond delay so that you can see what's happening before it happens. After you're done, you need to do the following. First, you need to compile your code using this hammer icon. To make sure that at all now here, as you can see, we have some errors. If we scroll here, you can see that the arrows here, we forgot the symbol on. Now, plus again on the Hummer, Michael. As you can see, we finished zero errors, the warnings and the top one second. Now you've done your codes right and you are ready to debug your code or run it on your board. And depending on the building will not have all that you have, you might do different configurations. Now, in my case, I will click here, run as the answer to Cortex and CC + + application. Now, you can also debug this code. Once you select this, let's go back here. But as I say, I'm 32, you will see this one too. Now, as you can see in this window, you can select the CC + + application, which is our application, the blank slate, the project name, you can select, that configuration you can select to enable Autobytel disable or Tobel use workspace settings.

You can go here to the debugger and select the debug probe. If you have a city link, you can choose it. If you have a still open positive version, you can select it from here. And if you have the J link, you can select it from here. Now, you can also start a local GDP server, but we can't really go. And change all of these configurations because different boards had different configurations and you have to check with a device manufacturer. Now, I don't have a link. So in this case, if you tried to upload the code and get the OK button, you would see that no stealing was detected. Please can still understand the boxes. So that's it. This is our first code. And feel free to write your board or your interface device so that I can help you upload, start and the bulk of code using your own board. I'm here to help you.

INTRODUCTION

We are a group of Chalfont engineers with one goal, which is to help you reach your full potential and microcontrollers and programming. This is our you dimmable file, we, well, skillful engineer who will deliver high quality courses for all of you from all around the world under the name of education engineering team, we work as a freelancer, engineering, helping a student in their graduation projects and give money courses about engineering topics.

We all want more than three websites, five blogs and two YouTube channels with more than two million views and 10000 subscribers. We use different ad networks and we have offered online courses for about five years now. We have more than 17 courses here at YouTube, me and many other courses on other platforms. As you can see, we have more than 5000 students and our course concentrates on electronics programming and microcontroller, as you can see here. And today, we are going to introduce you to how to use Michael C or C language and programming big microcontrollers. We will start with the basics and go from there so that you can create amazing coding, um, lines that will help you do exactly what you want as an outcome for your application.

OVERVIEW AND THE SOFTWARE TO BE USED

We will review basics and completion floor for sea labs, i.e., we will use the micro sea idea and then we will see. See extensions, in addition to that, we will see in-line assembly and interfacing with C. After that, we will be looking at examples, are we and Boynton's input output security? And functions and files, this is a quick overview of what we will take in this course. Let's talk about my trip to NYC among a lot of sea or a lot of High-Level languages. See is the closest to a similar language. It has many relation instructions and Boynton's for direct addressing. Most microcontrollers have available C compilers. The one we will be using is C or micro C. I will show you how to download it and how to use it. Writing in C simplifies code development for large projects. It makes it much easier. It helps you get the job done with a few lines of code and see the floor writing 101. You can do the very same code using ten lines in C language. Now this is a list of available C compilers, as you can see, Micros Hebrew, which is integrated and very sophisticated software on interface called integrated with the idea we have been using for labs. But I will shift to microsleep.

AVAILABLE C COMPILERS

* MikroC Pro – Integrated and very sophisticated Interface.

* Kiel – integrated with the IDE we have been using for labs.

* Reads51 – available on web site (http://www.rigelcorp.com/reads51.htm)

* Freeware: SDCC - Small Device C Compiler (http://sdcc.sourceforge.net/)

* Other freeware versions ...

Rule reads fifty one, which is available here free will such as the C, C small device compiler. You can get it from SourceForge, Botnet and a lot of other freeware versions. Now I will show you how to install C Blue, how to download it from the Internet and how to understand your PC so that you can be ready for the next Larsens. Let's head to the bazaar, right, Miklosi? Engorging. The first result is here, Michael Cebull, Fall-back, second bailout for microtia back my comptrollers, you can use it with other microcontrollers as well. But here I will be using this Kambala for see and generally to any microcontroller. Now, there is a download link, as you can see, this is it. When you click, download, download will begin to take about a minute. Let's see its features. As you can see, it supports sulphite controls. This is the March 24th, 2016 version, six point six point three. There have been improvements. This is its interface. I've been using it for two years now and I'm not having any problems. It's for operating systems and it has examples for beginners why you might choose this compiler.

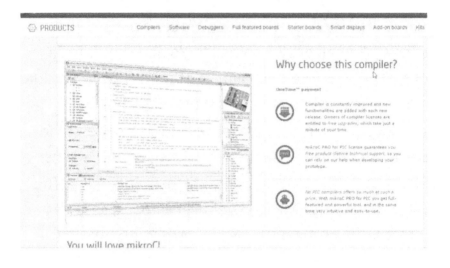

Why choose this compiler?

You will love mikroC!

It's constantly improving and new functionality is added. Uh, I second that since I download a new version each couple of months. As you can see, this is a single click, the bugging, you just need to click one button to get your hex file, which we'll talk about and listen to, also has a development board associated with it so you can develop your abs and test them in real life. Michael Courses is a very sophisticated software, so that's why I recommend it to you. OK, but I'm not finished. Double click on that thirty five. Then just keep clicking next. Next, I accept. Next, next, next, next. As you can see, it's extracting files. OK, here is a list of the files that are being extracted that are all microcontrollers files. These are support files for microcontrollers.

COMPILATION PROCESS AND YOUR FIRST C PROJECT

We will see different types of files created by Microsoft Software, IBM, the Lehman Files program to see when we compile it, we will save a project file called Mockbee and the combining process will generate a hex file that we can use with our microcontroller. Ferrol also and I simplified that will be created once we click on the CONMEBOL button or button. So this is the basic structure as you file a project file, hex file and assembly file, let's see these files and actions. Action. OK, now let's start, Michael, by clicking its icon on the desktop, or you can find it here and the start menu. OK, this is our user interface. Now let's create our first project file. You can click here and you project or find a new project. Let's name it the first lab. And let's talk in our portfolio. This is the main course, let's. Create a folder called Labs. Bloodborne. Now, this shows the boy's name, it's called, let's see, Unctuous Pig, 16 F.

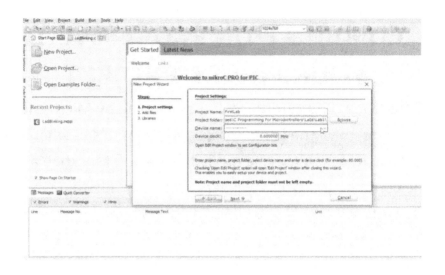

You don't have to do this, but you say, yes, we are using this and it's microcontroller based. We're not sure we need to choose a type for a controller. Now, click next. Do you want to clear this directory? Yes. Next, Next and finish. This is our main file first lab that we talked about here to see. Now, if we want the folder, we will see that there is a lab lab. We only have one filing first lab, the DCT. If we click on this button, CONMEBOL or Bell Bottom. It will ask us to save the first WSC file when we click on Save, it will generate a Hick's and a simplified version we collect here to build underbosses. As you can see, this is our assembly file, our C file, this is our Hick's font and this is our project file, all of these four files we talked about here in this. And this lesson, as you can see, is the time Scooby Doo takes us. Yes. Um, and, uh, our rainfall is that C we can open it using not bad and. Right.

Our second one. As you can see here, this is the code that exists here, and I want to see five.

HOW TO INCREASE THE FONT SIZE IN THE PROGRAMMING ENVIRONMENT

It's the most stable one. Then go to Tools options. Then go to the editor, as you can see here, a lot of stuff that is told, stuff about what we need a little tab, then click on Editors of Things. This one, Bob, click on Urban Options Dialogue.

Now, as you can see, here is a format button. If you click here, you will see that you can change the font type, style and size. I chose 16. You can choose more or less.

WHY C AND BASIC PROGRAM STRUCTURE

Well, modular programming is the answer. Like most high level languages, C is a modular programming language, but not an object oriented language. Each task can be encapsulated as a function. Entire program is encapsulated in the main function. To make this more clear, let's see the basic program structure. First, there are the compiler directives and include files. Then there is declaration of global variables and constants. After that, we have a declaration function. Then we have a main function, which we saw in the previous lesson, and we have some functions in addition to interrupt service routines. This is the basic structure of any C program. Now, an example. Let's see this blinking example. This is our main function that we talked about earlier. This is a definition of one of the bends. We are setting a leg or a bend or an output to be as an output note and what this is while one infinite loop. This is our code.

EXAMPLE: BLINKY.C

```c
void main()
{
    TRISB.F0 = 0; //Makes PORTB0 or RB0 Output Pin

    while(1) //Infinite Loop
    {
        PORTB.F0 = 1; //LED ON
        Delay_ms(1000); //1 Second Delay
        PORTB.F0 = 0; //LED OFF
        Delay_ms(1000); //1 Second Delay
    }
}
```

This piece of code will light a lid on this, will delay this, will light a lot of this, will delay. You don't need to understand this, but you have to see how this program is structured. This is the main function. These are. The limits, the beginning and the end, then we have all the beginning and the end, and this is the main code. This is a declaration sentence for the ban and this is a simple example of blinking a light that will turn off for a second, then turn on for a second and turn off and will continue to do that indefinitely. Now, let's get back to basics. All the programs consist of variables and functions. One of these functions must be the man so that the program can understand that this is the function to be executed first. And each function has statements inside it just like these. Line, these are called statements.

VARIABLES

all variables must be declared at the top of the program before the first statement declaration include type and list of variables, for example, FOID main void. Inside that we will write and we are. Kumah, tmb, then SeaMicro, these are two variables, and until they are declared as integrase, so we wrote in at the beginning when we wrote the name of each of these variables. Declaration of variables must be under the main function, cannot go outside. The main function must be inside it. So let's see different types of variables. That is the entire which is integrals. It has about 16 bits in our compiler. There is that child or character, it is eight bits there. Sure, it's about 16 bits.

- All variables must be declared at top of program, before the first statement.
- Declaration includes type and list of variables.
    Example: void main (void) {
                    int var, tmp; ——————— must go HERE!
- Types:
    - int (16-bits in our compiler)
    - char (8-bits)
    - short (16-bits)
    - long (32-bits)
    - sbit (1-bit) —————— not standard C – an 8051 extension
    - others that we will discuss later

And there is the long that 50 to. There are two bits here, and there is the last bit that takes only a single bit, one bit, and there are other variables that we will discuss later. Now, let's see, the foreign variable type can be signed or unsigned so the character can be signed or unsigned sign character it bits unsigned character also it bits. This one is from minus one hundred twenty two plus hundred twenty seven and four unsigned char. It will take from zero to plus 255 and the same goes for short and long, short and long. You should know the default is signed. It is best to specify if you are, if you need to understand how each of these were or if you know, uh, or if you suspect that any value will go in the minus, you need to specify the signed or unsigned char. You need to specify these in the right manner so that you will get the most accurate result. These are most mostly used in a calculator application using C language since science does matter. So you'll need to pay attention to these before writing your code. So before I think signed or unsigned, you need to understand the space that each of these occupies and the memory and the range of these values from where to where.

STATEMENTS AND OPERATORS

We will talk about statements, assignment's statement, we must write variable equals constant or extrapolation or variables. Example about equal 16 or 16 R equals O plus five J equals I. So there is a variable on the left side, as you can see here about I j and on the right side there is a constant 60 hour or expression like I plus five or a variable or variable like J equals I. These are three states of using variables. Now if we look at operators that is arithmetic. Operator plus minus multiplication and division, relational compression, larger, larger or equal, smaller, smaller, equal equality.

OPERATORS

- Arithmetic: +, -, *, /
- Relational comparisons: >, >=, <, <=
- Equality comparisons: ==, !=
- Logical operators: && (and), || (or)
- Increment and decrement: ++, --
- Example:

```
if (x != y) && (c == b)
{
    a=c + d*b;
    a++;
}
```

By comparison, does it equal or not equal logical operators such as and and or or. And there is also increment and decrement plus plus or minus minus an example. This is a quick example of using operators. If we wrote this, if the statement if X doesn't equal Y and C equals B, then do the following. So if these two statements are true, it will execute the following. If none of them were false, it won't execute anything. So if we need to execute this, if any of this is true, we can use or C and this is a logical situation here and I want that. I want to explain since it's really simple and, uh, to fit, the conditions must be met where or if any one of the conditions are met, it will execute the code. Now, let's look at bitwise logic instruction. And this is a sign and this is an example, unequals and zero X of zero or this is a sign X or as you can see, left and right shift, left shift will move the value to the left, uh, right shift will move the value to the right first complement. Well, um, let's say will. It will basically, uh, change or reverse the value. So if it's won, it will be zero zero, it will be won. So it's, uh, reversing values.

BITWISE LOGIC INSTRUCTIONS

		Examples:
• AND	&	$n = n \mathbin{\&} 0xF0;$
• OR	|	
• XOR	^	
• left shift	<<	$n = n \mathbin{\&} (0xFF << 4)$
• right shift	>>	
• 1's complement	~	$n = n \mathbin{\&} \sim(0xFF >> 4)$

So if we wrote it before, no, let's say one zero one zero, the result will be zero one zero one. This is a very simple example of using this first compliment and a compliment. Word means that each zero will be won and each one will be zero. An example, logic and a simple answer. Let's keep that seat aside. This is our voice, man. We are defining a variable called x, char, x, x, equal X. As you can see this sign we just talked about, it's X or then X equals X or zero zero C, X equals X and zero X FC, then B zero equals X zero is board zero. Here we will send X value to about zero. We kind of live the same thing using assembly, but I want to explain it since we are talking about see only here. But this is a nice way to compare these two cos they produce the same result. But as you can see this is and isn't really user friendly. X are all or and all you need to have another XI to be able to write on a simple code or you need to have a very good memory now and that will talk about lub statements. And while if you didn't understand variables, unsettlement very well you will understand them well once we write our first code using microtia environment.

LOOP STATEMENTS

Now we will talk about LUB statements, we will start with why Leupp, why has this structure while between two, as you can see here? We must try the condition, then we must try the statement. You should use these signs only. This one is for conditions and this one is a false statement or quote. One condition is a true execution statement. If there is only one statement, we can lose the practice. Example, with one semicolon, this will loop the court forever. So if we write a statement inside two brackets after one one, it will loop it forever. Now, let's see the second one, which is for statement for first, we must try initialization, then a condition, then an increment, then we can write the code between all the statements between these two practices: initialization done before a statement is executed, condition is tested. If true, execute statements, do incremental steps and go back and test the condition again. Repeat the last two steps until the condition is not true.

LOOP STATEMENTS - FOR
* For statement:

for (initialization; condition; increment) {statements}

initialization done before statement is executed

condition is tested, if true, execute statements
do increment step and go back and test condition again

repeat last two steps until condition is not true

This is, uh, declared for repeated Manon's with a condition and initialization. And this is a simple example for using a for loop. Here our variable equals zero. This is the condition and is less than one thousand. Then the increment is and plus plus plus plus means unequals and plus one or means and uh all means increment one to the end value. Be careful with signing into Gaza. You must take very good care of these. So this is another code for all equals zero. All but less than thirty three thousand. Then the increment is a loss led equals not let's not let. Here is the complement that we talked about in the previous lesson. It will reverse the set of this variable that is called. So if it's one it will be zero zero. It will be one. Why is this an infinite loop? Well, you need to answer this question and write your answer in case you aren't able to and you might get a chance to win a free one for all of my other courses. Now, the last. Lube is the why loop do the understatement then, while the exhibition is dismayed at the bottom of the top of the loop. So this statement is executed once before this thing, the condition. So this is the difference between the wild and wild and why loop, which is the condition, then execute the statement while in the wild we execute the statement at least once, then we check the condition.

CONDITIONS IF AND SWITCH

Now, let's talk about if statements and decision making, if the statement is really simple, if the condition, then a statement or else if another condition, then another statement, then it keeps going, else statement and so on. So we need to write this condition and we write our statement according to this condition. Another type of decision making in three languages: which statement, switch expression, then there is our case. We have a constant here, then our statement, then another case, Cornerstone's statement, then the default statement. Now, to understand this, we need to see an example. Let's see an example switch case here. If this value equals zero zero zero, then return this value. If this value or this variable equals zero X1 01, then return this value.

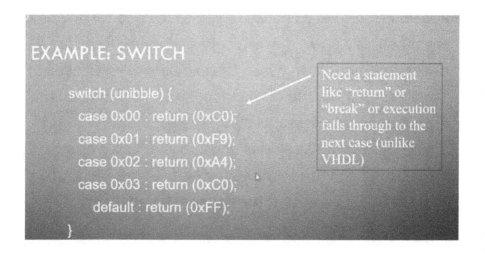

EXAMPLE: SWITCH

```
switch (unibble) {
    case 0x00 : return (0xC0);
    case 0x01 : return (0xF9);
    case 0x02 : return (0xA4);
    case 0x03 : return (0xC0);
    default : return (0xFF);
}
```

Need a statement like "return" or "break" or execution falls through to the next case (unlike VHDL)

If this unit variable equals zero zero two zero X, if all it needs are statements like return or break or execution for the next case, unlike the other. So if we don't try to return or break here, it will go from case one to case two. It won't execute anything here and it won't stop here if this condition is met. So you need to take good care of this, not now. Before going any further, I need to show you how we can use F and switch statements and A Michael C, which is conditioning so that you can understand it more. Let's define two variables and X equals zero and Y equals zero because now let's combine our code to ensure that we have no errors. OK? There are no errors, as you can see. Now, there's one thing that is really beautiful about Michael's environment. If there is an error, we don't try to Mickleham here and we comply. The court will tell us that there is a syntax error as is expected here. So once you put it back you can compile your code. Now let's see if X equals Y, I need you. To increase by one. This is a simple code as an example for using if we need another condition, we got a lot else if. As you can see, we cannot light another condition that doesn't equal why? We need to reduce exposure, not increment declarant by one X equals X minus one, as you can see here, and so on. This is for if statements. Now, what about switch statements? Let's see the ICOM light switch. Switch X now if you kiss one. X equals X plus one. Then break the case too. X equals X plus two. Then break. Default. Rick. OK, now we come to this break something. Now let's call our code.

```
     void main() {

         int x=0;
         int y=0;

         if(x==y)
         {
         x=x+1;
10       }else if(x!=y)
         {
         x=x-1;
         }


16       switch (x)
         {
         case 1: x=x+1; break;
         case 2: x=x+2; break;
20       default: break;
         }
     }
```

This is our switch statement, which means we want to
scan the variable X. If its value equals one, then increment
X by one. If X value equals two, then increment its value
about two, then break Blic means get out of switch since
the condition met. So you must write it or else the code
will continue running and will go on to scan the next case
below the first scale that we just executed. These are the

if statement on the switch that if all scales and the switch statements which are used for conditions.

NUMBERING SYSTEM

We will talk about a very important thing, which is numbering systems. As most of you know, there are a lot of numbering systems, including this amount of hexadecimal binary and octal decimal today. I will talk to you about decimal hexadecimal and binary to start a new project. Choose Arnebeck. Let's say that from to. For next next finish now, in Michael's environment, the default numbering system is dismal. So if I wrote all the find a new variable, let's say integer equals zero. This means that the variable A has a decimal value of zero. If I want to write it in hexadecimal, I must define that. I want to use hexadecimal by starting with the zero zero zero. This means that I am using hexadecimal. As you can see here. If I want to write the number in binary, I must write. This. Fix there will be. Eight numbers. Now, why do we have two numbers here while here at number? This is a binary number. So each hexadecimal number has an associated four by nine numbers. Now, if you want to see this in action, Michael, environment, provide a quick convertor. So if you're not zero here, it will equal zero zero and hexadecimal and it will equal eight zeros and binary. So this is a very easy way to do this if we wrote it once. As you can see here, the equals 255 and it equals, uh, and decimal and equals half of hexadecimal. So you can use any of these as you can, as we said earlier, the default as decimal. So we don't need a better fix for the decimal system. But in the case of hexadecimal or binary, we need zero Axford hexadecimal zero B for binary. This is really important. A really important thing that you must take into consideration now. If. I wrote four ones here, as you can see, for ones equals F and decimal equals 15. Now, how can we convert from buying those two decimals? I can show you a quick explanation on how to do this. Now, let's say that we have one one, one, one. These are the four ones that are written here. And in order to convert this into this, we must write the value of each bet one to four. Eight. Now, one, two, four, eight, 16, 32, 64, and go on, uh, for once means that we need some one plus two plus four plus eight, which equals 15 here. Now, if one of these numbers is zero, we will cancel the associated value. So we will have some one plus two equals three plus eight equals 11.

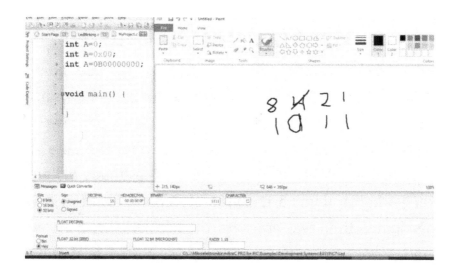

As you can see here, only the one with ones must be calculated. Let's try one one zero here and see if it will equal 11 or not. As you can see here, it equals 11, just like we started here. It's a really simple method, you just need to write one, two, four, eight, 16, 32, 64 and assign ones and zeroes. OK, that's it for the numbering system. I recommend using the converter since you won't have to do this process, but you need to understand how this is done. Uh, you can choose to use the semantics of this amount or binary in case you want specific control board bins. You need to use binary since it allows you to control eight bends. So we started one here and one here. This means that we are controlling two bands of the board. The same can be done here and here. But this gives you flexibility in handling numbers.

USING OPERATORS

We will talk about operators and how we can use them and our code. Let's start by writing a few statements if. Let's say that these numbers are A, B, C, and let's give them different values, zero, one and two for the sake of this example. Now. Let's. Still, some things that will help you get better if you are using if statements start by doing this right, if then two brackets, then to curly brackets, you need to do this so that you won't miss any bracket and you won't have to trace an error if you did. Next thing is going here with your mouth and writing your first operator example. Let's say if A equals B, now inside this, we would say that increase by one error plus plus this sentence all equals eight equals eight plus one. So if we are writing this sentence, let's say. This equals being equal, a plus one that we can see here. This is the same as this. So if these two variables and B are equal, it will, uh, cut out this code, another use is greater. So if A is greater or equal, B, it will, uh, execute this code smaller than, um, there is also no equal, which is this sine. Um. Other operators are, let's say that if we are not equals A, this means invert, invert or try to find the complement of A.. So if it equals one, it will be zero. If it equals zero, it will be one we talked about earlier. But we are talking about again, so that you can so that you know that this is really important. You need to know how to handle these things. If you're not only one equals sign, this sentence will be logically wrong, since we are equal in two values, not asking if they are equal to each other. So you need to double equal. So, uh, so that this sentence will ask if A equals B.. This means does equal B if we wrote this, this means that these both the value of B inside A this is really important. You shouldn't miss out on it.

Uh, another important note is that if you want to keep track of your practices and practices, uh, you need, uh, to click here. Biomorphs. This is the opening. This is the end.

This is the opening of the girl brackets and this is the end. Uh, this is right for the operators. You can use the word inside any condition and you can write multiple conditions. Now, if we want to apply multiple conditions here, we can understand A equals C, does it equal C? This means that these two conditions must meet so that this code can be executed. If we want the code to be executed with one of these conditions through, we must try it or. This means or so if this is true or if this is true, it will execute this code, um, it's fairly simple

USING FUNCTIONS

We will talk about functions, functions are very. Productive method for making the code simpler. This is a function, it's called void man. Once you create a new project, you will find it there. The man means that this is the main function of our program and the code written inside it will be executed. First void means that this function doesn't return anything. If you see these two brackets empty, this means that this function doesn't take. And what this is the first time functions, the one that doesn't return anything and doesn't take. And so what is the second time you ask? Well, sometimes the ones that return things but don't take input. Uh, first we will start by the variable that this function returns variable time. Let's say that to an integer value. Let's name it some and. As you can see, two practices and two Calibra since. This is our new function, if we had compiled, you will see that, let's say let's see this early and it is far defined, OK? He is stating that he is redefining the standard. See? As we can see now, everything is working correctly now and some this function doesn't take in between these two brackets, but it will return an integral value if you change this, to float, to return a float value, if you change it to string, it will return a string value string and it's strong. Let's get it back to Antigo. Now, let's say that I want to define two variables and each one equals one. And let's define them up there. You see, let's look at some of the variables. There's some plus B. And C one equals A plus B. OK, now let's compare the calls so that everything's fine, C one equals A plus B. This will sum the two variables and B and sort of the result in C one, we want to return C one value. We must try to return C one then combine.

```
void main()
{



}

int sum()
{
c1=A+B;
return c1;
}
```

This method. Is the second time to take anything but put it in and take our value by using the term, then the variables, the variable that it's thought is Antigo, you can't use string variable here or float variable. You must use the very same type of variable stated before the function. And this can be changed to anything. You can name it educational. As you can see, you can do it with your name, say anything can be used, how can we call this function the main function? You just need to call it by its name. And as you can see here, we call it, but we don't have the order to store water to return to us. So let's define a new variable and the result equals zero. Now, if we start to see a result, equal mud, the result of something zero plus one equals one. It will return one. Once we call it here, this variable will equal one. So this is the second type of function. Now, let's look at the third time. It's really similar to the second time, except for the fact that it will take and what. And one. And two. OK, let's, uh. I want to hear and five them up there and the variable section. It all says that this will equal zero and this will equal to for the sake of this example. Now, this. Some estimate, some will take to Antigua's, the 100 to. And will some of them understand the results and see one, then it will let them see one? As we stated here, the difference between this one and this one is that this method will take two and both under the term of value. This will take no input, but it will return a value.

DIGITAL INPUTS AND DELAY LOOPS

I will talk about switches, digital imports and the ELOPES switches on understanding both are basically the same for every microcontroller. If you want a kind of switch, you should write an if statement asking whether that switch is closed or open, then execute a code. Depending on that, uh, it will basically count on digital inputs. So you assign inputs or from both pens and your controller and you'll steer them. Today I will talk about BigMac controller, uh, in order to assign a board to support A or B as in, but we must use a register called Tressell or trust B after that we can ask if bought a, let's say, dot of zero, which means the first Barnawartha equals zero or one executes the following code. Let's see this in action. We must first say here, press a equals zero zero zero f f. This means all of the events are in, but now the of statement. Between the two brackets ask if a bit of zero equals one, then execute the following code, let's say it's a one, C one equals one plus two. OK, now let's see two. OK, let's try to see two. Yeah. As you can see, if, uh, we clicked on, uh, bought a lot of zero, which is the first Penenberg in my controller, let's see it here. This has brought us a simulation environment. OK, let's create a new project next, next. Finish now three other big 16 F. 84. That's it. These men are e0, we never hear of this board, which was bought from Orazio 34 is called bought here.

Start Page   LedBlinking.c   MyProject.c

```c
void main()
{
    TRISA=0b11111111;

    if(porta.f0==1)
    {
        c2=a1+a2;
    }

}
```

Messages   Quick Converter

☑ Errors	☑ Warnings	☑ Hints	
Line	Message No.		Message Text
0	1144		Used RAM (bytes): 8 (15%) Free RAM (bytes): 44 (85%)
0	1144		Used ROM (program words): 42 (4%) Free ROM (program words): 982 (96%)
0	125		Project Linked Successfully

If we need to assign if it spends as input or output, we must use Thrissur just for more flexibility in assigning the values we can avoid. It'll be one one, one one. As you can see, one means both. If we're not zero here, this means that the board will be out. But let's give it one. This is the first thing that I want to talk about, this is what this sentence is used for, assigning digital inputs, and this is for scanning a specific board pen if it has a specific value to execute this code. Those are the things that are called delay loops. If we want to add a delay or time for us to examine certain things, such as lighting a red door, rotating a mortar, we can avoid delay. I'm asked and I must stand for milliseconds. This is underscore. And we cut out a hundred or let's say a thousand milliseconds, which means a second, we can use us, which stands for Michael. So you can sue us and case multiplexing for us for a millisecond. So you have us and us, each of them once four microseconds. And the other one or the other one is four milliseconds.

THE THINGS THAT YOU NEED

I'll be showing you all through the series of the video what are the components that you need to program a desk to enter into a microcontroller. So this is the microcontroller that we need. And you'll be used to out a series of the whole truth. The whole video is the entry to EF 1 0 3 C eighty six microcontroller so is not commonly known as blue pill. You can buy from China or eBay or anywhere. And therefore the programmer and debugger. This is the thing that will be used to program and debug the microcontroller. Okay. And that one is the FP FTB program. Okay. So this after the programmer will be used to the bar.

What is happening in the microcontroller and you can send a message to a serial timer because this is stealing the debugger . It doesn't provide a way to send a message to the CEO. I mean no I will be using these FTT programmer and then these are the three basic things that you need for now and for now to do some simple programming for the first maybe first few videos you need these trainings back as I go further into the into the idea project you might need the more complicated components and right now assume that you already have all the basic components such as the Breitbart racist the LCD potential meet the push button. I assume that you could have all this already. And so right now these are treating the microcontroller, the debugger and the FTB I program. These are the three basic things that you need on this project.

MICROPROCESSOR VS MICROCONTROLLER

The difference between microprocessor and microcontroller is that I get it from the my which is developed by the steam I created electronic so uh in this is the architecture of the microcontroller. So these context entry over here needs context. Entry is a microprocessor as micro electronics. They bought the microprocessor cortex incremental processor from the company. So this is a company okay. And then they in the integrate e with other things like flash memory the GPI or ADC and a. All these things.

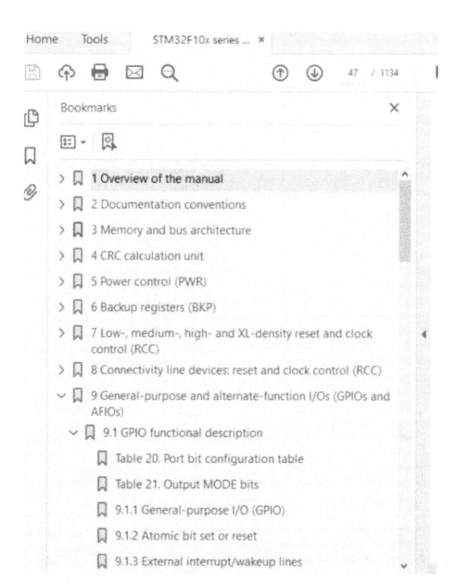

Bookmarks   ×

– AHB to APBx (APB1 or APB2), which connect all the APB peripherals

These are interconnected using a multilayer AHB bus architecture as shown in *Figure 1*:

Figure 1. System architecture (low-, medium-, XL-density devices)

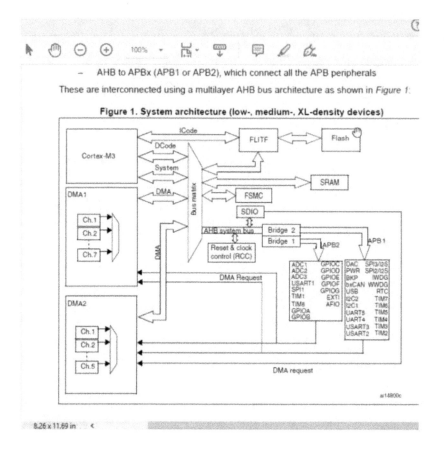

And then maybe into a microcontroller. So these cortex and creates a business. This whole thing is a microcontroller. All right. So we have two companies that got involved in it. And then the other company bought the microcontroller. So we look at this one the blue blue that we are going to use in the media and in the project of the other company. Maybe this company bought the blue beer from China. So that's a Chinese company. By the microcontroller from SD microelectronics and then maybe into a development board by routine external

Christo the U.S. interface the debug interface and the media into a bot and sell to us.

KEIL UVISION IDE SETUP

So right now you have to click on a project and open up the microfiche idea. Click on a project click new micro Vision project and right now you can see it as any name I would say the file name is set up safely. And then I would just add a microcontroller. That coming for Steve microelectronics F1 series F1 0 3 and that's 1 0 to see it. Okay. So this might just be one click So I will need two packages. One is to call from the senses and then the other one is the device start up. So you just need these two packages to do some basic programming on the microcontroller. So I will be discussing the other uh packages in the future. OK right now go to target in the source Group 1. Here is where we create our main file. So right click click a new item to group to create a mean file. Chris you will use the C program to program uh the entry. So give it a name. I won't name you. I mean I O K so right now I view that project so I do the project you release all the files that you need like the hate file. Okay. I know you can see that there's a hater file. This is because I hate the fact that we need it in our main c file. So in order to include the hateful the s that include the entity to f once your eggs don't hatch and then they have a main function. That's our main function so call my probation. Uh required us to add a new line here. Otherwise it would give us a warning message. Mean bureau project.

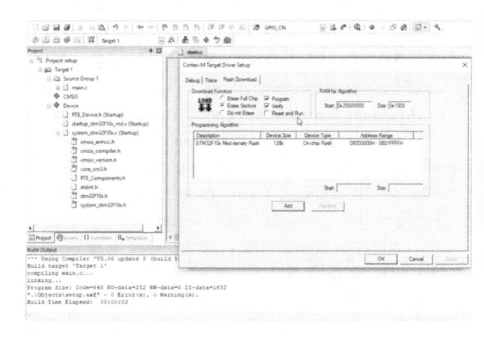

So right now you can be at Project um before we program we need to configure the debugger so go to flash configure slash DOS go to the bar reduce the debugger. In my case if they're stealing me back. And then go to settings to make sure that is the port missed. Oh here is the establishment instead of G10. Okay. And then go to flash download. We need to slow this reset and run okay. Is that when you upload it? Right. That's when I blew a program. We played a reset and the program would run automatically if you don't click check it. You had to press the reset button manually yourself in order to run a program on your microcontroller. So right now I clearly first and then actually the flash memory for that or this or my microcontroller is this I should be 1 0 it should be 64 64 kilobytes. Okay so it is the size I change it to 1 instead of 2. So right now click Okay. And then this is the external Crystal frequency you would be in my megahertz and then right now dicey for the basic configuration right now. Compute it to a program.

USE KEIL UVISION FOR DEBUGGING

So let's see if you have read some quotes and then a quote that you have written. It doesn't mesh what you want it to happen so you can use a comic revision to Iraq to see what is happening to no wearable place and register what's going on right. So you can copy the code that is written. We have configured the GBI 0 for the enable the J O.S. 13 wishes on what LCD On your mark on your entry to what. And this is a wearable cow and the string wearable. Right now I would do it yes no problem there's no error. I'll go into a debug session so all we can do is that. So let's say we want to see what is happening to your wearable right. So by now I can actually put a breakpoint over here okay. And then I can click on the cow and then right click on the cow to watch one. Wash 1 is a place for you to see what is happening to your wearable right. Right click it.

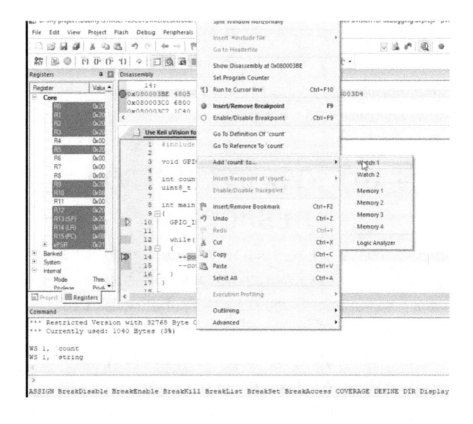

So moving right now you can see that it is in recess. So the value is it is in noisy value or not I run it so it goes to zero because you have initialized the cow as a global robo with zero and then I run it because I put a breakpoint over here so you stop at this point so you can see that right now the arrow is pointing towards this line right. So when the arrow is pointing towards this line it means that it has been running this line of code just at this time. So to run this line of code plus plus the cow you can go to this one that over. So when you press it is over. Jenny runs this line of code and goes through this line. So right now you can press that over so you can see that the cow goes to 1. So then you can rest a step over again. You can see that because minus minus cow the cow right now goes back to zero. And are you going to present it plus minus plus minus. Right and this is how you use a wash to see what is happening to the cow. So wearable. You can also use the wash window to see the string value so we can see that I have initialized the string if drawing the string where we have a string. Oh hello. Okay. Open the string variable and see that at each memory base. At restoring one by one. Hell You can also see the string. You can see the individual variable and you can see whatever variable you have into it right. And then the next thing is if you want to see what is happening to the register. So let's right now reset it again. Okay and go to you can put a three point edit by night vision. Oh yeah. Go to the Paris house system view over RCC. So in this RCC. Right. It shows all the registered days long RCC. So I have configured this register APB to be an hour. So this register is used to enable the clock for the proxy so we can see the moment when I run it. Right. So is it an issue of values. Is zero the recent value is zero. So go to Ashley you can see that this is the APB to our register. So the recent rally we see is zero. So the moment I reset the value of zero and then I run it comes to this line at this moment in heaven. As you get this quote The moment that I rest that over you can see that right now APB an r e. Me or the policy is enabled. Right. So right now you can see what's happening in the register. Value anything you know. And you are able to see what is actually happening in your code by looking at the register and how to see the register. I not only object to the agenda. Maybe you can say that if you want to see ABC you can see the ABC register as a list of ABC one register. Maybe go to SBI agency on May 17 to adjust their menu and next time you want it. Right. You can put a brake voice or big points and then run the code line by line and then you can see what is happening to your register value and you can print out what is the problem with your code. And the last thing that you can do is that and go to the system again GPI.

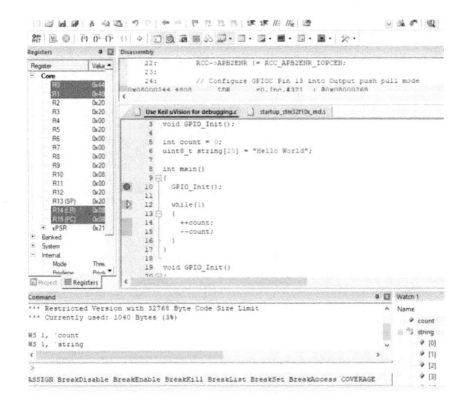

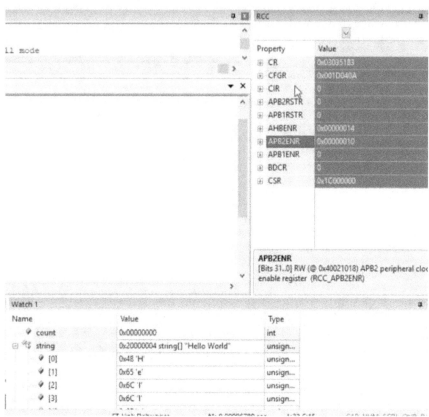

Property	Value
⊞ CR	0x03035183
⊞ CFGR	0x001D040A
⊞ CIR	0
⊞ APB2RSTR	0
⊞ APB1RSTR	0
⊞ AHBENR	0x00000014
⊞ APB2ENR	0x00000010
⊞ APB1ENR	0
⊞ BDCR	0
⊞ CSR	0x1C000000

APB2ENR
[Bits 31..0] RW (@ 0x40021018) APB2 peripheral clock
enable register (RCC_APB2ENR)

Watch 1

Name	Value	Type
◆ count	0x00000000	int
⊟ string	0x20000004 string[] "Hello World"	unsign...
◆ [0]	0x48 'H'	unsign...
◆ [1]	0x65 'e'	unsign...
◆ [2]	0x6C 'l'	unsign...
◆ [3]	0x6C 'l'	unsign...

Oh I see. If I want to toggle them out. Right. So there's a checkbox over here or the our so that all our register when you set it right you can actually set or reset. You can actually toggle the pin high low or low too high. OK so this or that we lost a bet. We'll see. And in 30 Juba OCP in Turkey belonged to the LTTE on the east and they did both. So the moment when I press it I should be able to toggle the LTTE so that right now when I say us First I write a code. I know that you get all the initialization. We run them and I press you about getting or the tracking I can actually call go out on my board. You can connect your microcontroller to your computer. You can Pogo yourself to see what's happening and this is how you use all this method to be about what is happening with your code.

USE STM STUDIO FOR DEBUGGING

You can copy and edit the main function. I have configured 60 config to generate an interrupt for every one millisecond so that interrupt name is Assistant handler for everyone. One millisecond you enter this interrupt and increase this and as it becomes wearable. And this is a delay. Maybe a second function in a while loop. I have put 30 so these to generate a tiny millisecond delay and then everything that a millisecond delay it will increase the cow and the cow one variable. So right now I will. Beautiful and then go into my board. So right now I will go to the esteemed studio so you can download it. Is that the dance to do? You can go to Google such as dance studio and scroll to the bottom. You can get software over here. And in this web site you can get a selfie over here and I will not go through how to download it. I believe it is easy to download. So right now once you download the file you can open it up. So right now go to file input variable juiced the file go to the right now and go to the location where you create your project. I'll go to see the and ask the entity to scratch and this is the place where I treat my project and then go to go to a place with a creative project click on it click on the object and then click the x s file and select and then what I want is this to wearable I want to see what is happening with these two rebel and then you can click on the import right now you can just bang the wearable settings that do wearable that you want to wash and then you can pull it towards you drag it to us here. So right now I have the President reset button on my as the entry to board and then the court right now is running. The program is running on the display. You can actually see the wearable and what's going on with the wearable using a curve or bar graph or table.

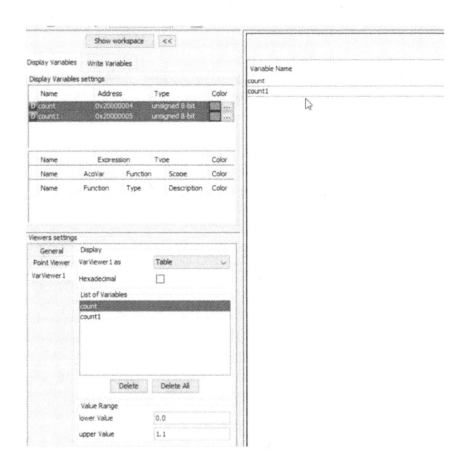

VarViewer1

Address/Expression	Read Value
0x20000004	59
0x20000005	59

So I see in table form right now less running. So you can see that the count is increasing and the count is also increasing. I see. And then let's say if you want to stop now okay. You can see that if you press on this box the Cal value stops increasing by the count one still increasing. So the program is running back there. However Bill Judy stops so you can actually modify the value inside and say I want to modify it to become fi and then press Enter so you can see that a cow and a cow one value is different right now. All right, so let's stop it right now. Go to file go to Options acquisition settings. So over here in the acquisition barometers these log files. So the moment when you get the data from Colorado you start in this log file. So this is the location of my log file. I copy. Open it. So these log files and I get away. So right now you can see that you have to wearables cow and cow on this list that here is the time a millisecond so you can see that these the value of the counting cow on or in log files so let's say maybe next time you have your gyro you can actually use the curve OK to see what is what is happening with the angle of the gyro. So it's actually a very great tool for you to see what is happening to the variables in pulse.

INPUT MODE SCHMITT TRIGGER

So when you come to us this is the entry to Ashleigh in the input configuration. Chapter 9. Page 163. You can't see this figure. And it has the input driver. And over here is the input pin and the input pin the data that comes towards this input pin. You go through the speed trigger before being read by the CB you. So when the king of the microcontroller is being program X. input this mi trigger is activated by default. You don't have to activate it manually. And over here is the output driver. That's a switch over here. It says that when the input part of an input pin is configured as input the switch is disabled. So when you say anything in the output that is just the data there won't be any effect on the pin because this fish right now over here is already being disabled. I explain the case where the microcontroller doesn't have a smooth trigger when the microcontroller let's say it does not have the speed trigger in and then it might only have a single track so it means that random microcontroller sees that no wattage and a microcontroller pin is higher than one point seven Volt and then the thing by the microcontroller is one way or if the voltage is lower than one point seven will the state read by the microcontroller is zero. So let's consider this diagram at t 1 when the voltage at the microcontroller pin goes from 0 and greater than one point seven Volt right now at t1 the step by the microcontroller is 1 it will change to 1 when we didn't win by 7. And then as long as is in a bullfight by 7 ball the state read by the microcontroller will be 1 and then at t 2 Over here then the voltage and microcontroller P is slightly below 1 by 7 will read by the microcontroller now goes back to 0 and then it became 0 until the voltage at the microcontroller being goes both 1 by 7. So there will only be a single trestle and this is the key that we don't want it to happen because at this point at T2 and T tree this is the noise that caused the voltage and the microcontroller to be lowered more than one point seven.

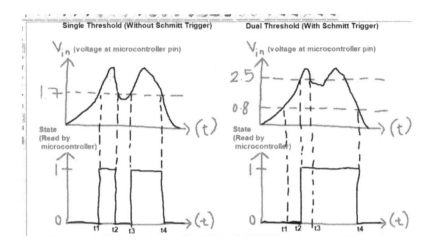

And then it costs the state read by the microcontroller to false from one and then goes to zero and then it goes back to one again. And this is what we do one and to solve this problem we need to have a smooth trigger install. So here is a bit of an enhancement trigger but this is the website that I found on Google. So this January is so good on how they actually designed a smart trigger. We don't have to really understand the second part of the trigger. We just need to know actually and it comes with dual trestle. It means that only when the voltage at the microcontroller goes below 2.5 full and then the state of the microcontroller change to 1 and if the voltage at the microcontroller being goes below zero point eight Well let's say and then on the state of the microcontroller goes to zero and the value of the trash so it depends on how the designer designed a circuit of symmetry trigger and it's not actually stated in the data sheet so I will just assume it will be 2.5 and zero point eight. So right now let's say a T1 is the voltage at the microcontroller he goes above zero point eight will the state of the microphone control every means zero. Only at T2 when the voltage at the microcontroller beam goes up 2.5. And then you will change to one. So right now even at this point that's a noise over here and makes the voltage and the microcontroller being below 2.5 for the state of the microcontroller right now. It doesn't change. It retains at one only. At this point P4 when the voltage at the microcontroller pin goes below zero point eight will you only change to zero. This is the advantage of having a smooth trigger as if you remove noise something like this when the voltage goes below 2.5 will you also retain the S1 and this is what you call hysteresis effect. The State of the microcontroller will only change when it goes above or below a certain threshold. So let's consider the rate line which is that at the SSD it is the voltage at the microcontroller and the y axis is the state bit by the microcontroller. So when the voltage at a microcontroller pin goes above 2 by 5 4 it will only change to 1 and then consider the yellow line when the voltage slowly changes from 2 by 5 4 and then goes below 2.5 for and then goes 0 0 0 by 8 mode. You will only change when it goes below zero point APR and recalls this as a hysteresis effect as it will retain.

INPUT MODE PULL UP, PULL DOWN, FLOATING MODE

I explain about who oppresses the pull down resistor and floating in the pool when the microcontroller pin is configured as input, not so in the input configuration of these that Ashley so he can see in the input driver of the assembly to use this might. And here is what the resistor and pulled out is. So notice that there's a switch for a pull up and decimal switch for the pull down while you configure your microcontroller as a pull up this switch to be turned on and this situation will be turned off by you continually a microcontroller s pull now this fish turn off and this fish turn on. So here is the white racist and the rest is the rising star and a floating input. So in the pool resistor when you configure the microcontroller in the input mode with a port resistor you can use it as fish and the switch is connected to the ground. Once our issues connected to the ground and one side was connected to the pin. So this P is originally pulled up to the BBC so the microcontroller reads the pin as high.

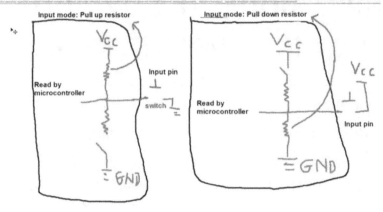

Input mode: Pull up resistor

Input mode: Pull down resistor

V_{CC}

V_{CC}

V_{CC}

Input pin

Read by microcontroller

Read by microcontroller

switch

GND

Input pin

GND

When the user presses fraiche and then the current flow from the VTC to the ground and the p read by the microcontroller is 0 and then you can figure that microcontroller as pull down the pull up stage is turn off and pull down which is turned on it's close. You can see here and right now you can use it in Swedish. Once our station is connected to the ICC and once that is connected to the pin. So right now because he's pulling down the pin originally read by the microcontroller is zero. When the switch is pressed right now the current will flow from the BTC to the ground being read by the microcontroller right now.

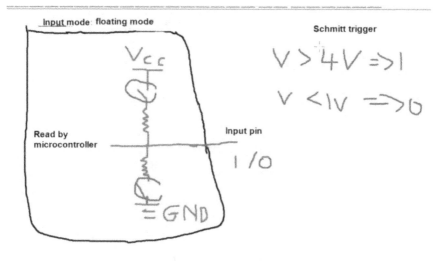

Input mode: floating mode

Read by microcontroller

V_{cc}

Input pin

I/O

GND

Schmitt trigger

$V > 4V \Rightarrow 1$

$V < 1V \Rightarrow 0$

High if you configure your microcontroller as a floating most poor upstage and pulled out fish is turn off the wall dish read by the microcontroller at the input pin is unable to determine we don't know that whether the pin is 1 0 0 in the last several videos I've explained about might trigger when the voltage at the pin is greater and follow the judiciary by the microcontroller is one if the voltage at the input P is smaller than one wall and then it will be considered as 0 microcontroller as 0. So this is how the port receives the address the. And the throttling is more used in the microcontroller.

OUTPUT MODE OPEN DRAIN CONFIGURATION

Can you just set it to input more or you can say yes I'll put more so when you set it to output more you can actually set it into open green mode or push pull mode. So I would be talking about the open green mode. This is a register inside that microcontroller that you can set to be 1 0 0 0 when you set it to be zero. The V is equal to zero and you set it to one and end up being equal to 1. So let's say when it comes to this register the output that I register right so for this register is the register that you set the pin it represented as V in over here. All right. It is represented as being so let's say if you are setting pin 13 is equal to zero. We could zero over here if you set a pin that is equal to

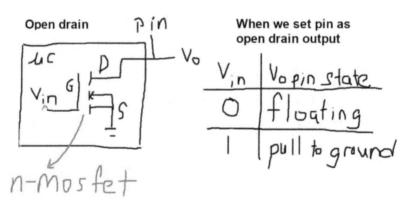

V_{in}	V_o pin state
0	floating
1	pull to ground

Conclusion: We can only pull the Pin down to ground, we cannot pull the pin up to high (Vcc). For example, we cannot blink LED.

1. The V is equal to 1 and then let's say you set a V in equal to zero this. This thing is the most packed trains. It's a more spec and more spec and set it to zero. This most Fed will be kind of because the gate the voltage of the gate the respect to S is zero. So it will not turn on the most fact it turn off the most fact and then right now you can assume that this peak this line right here can assume that this line right here is actually cut off. So when this line right here is cut all the pin is actually floating is connected no nothing. So when it's connected or nothing if there's an electrical noise or something that's a noise that let you affect the output. So the P E means the ground or high. So we call it exploding. So let's say instead of being a good one and most effect will be on so when it is turned on. This whole line is actually you can assume that this order is actually connected and the ping is actually pulled to ground is connected to ground because it pulls the ground. So there are only two states one is quoting state and one is pulled to ground. It depends on the beat that you set in the register. So we can conclude that we can only pull the pin down by setting the V in equal to one and we cannot pull the pin high. So which means that we cannot set blink out. We cannot said that we need to be kind of high and there's not much thing that we can do with the output more open v output more. So right now in order to let's say if you wonder bling it out. Right. You want to say that we need to become high. You want to use our application. We we

have to use a register. So this is I have a draw near ready so if you want to steady high obviously and then you want to set it low you can actually add internal internal register or external register. So let's say in our application again we have four and more right over here. This is a B which is the beat that we set in the output register over here and then right now let's say this is an internal activity internal White resistor. This is a racist. Okay. Over here. This is a racist. This is internal who oppresses the is connected to the we call we pull out because over here. This. No. This no one is actually connected to the VTC is who is up to the race to see and then right now let's see if we use it in the application. Right. Is that our idea of progress is the most right? The moment when you said let's say over the. In this would like to register the moment they said zero they would be as good as zero. These trends that most stay and most bang are actually turned off. So this connection is broken So then the cease is broken. Right now the visa is the current U.S. law in this way. And then the LGB will be turned on. All right. I do it. And then lastly when you send the V in equal to one we go to one. This most fact will be turned on. So when these must be turned on the current that will be connected to ground over here is actually indirectly connected to the ground. So Karen instead of flowing here instead of flowing here right now it flows here. So right now the LTTE will actually be pulled to ground. So right now we can say that the LTTE is either Pu up to the. When we go to zero it is put up to the VTC in which there is a good one that is put at the ground right by using it in Denmark. What is the same goes to the open drain with external powers.

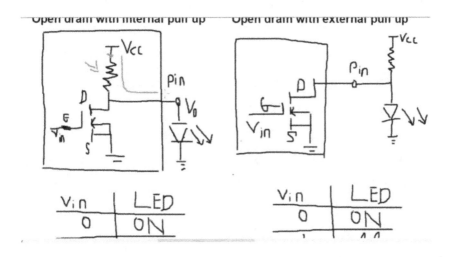

Open drain with internal pull up   Open drain with external pull up

Vin	LED
0	ON

Vin	LED
0	ON

So this internal piracy that is inside a microcontroller, this external power register is outside microphones outside the microcontroller. So let's say if you don't activate it you don't want to activate the internal resistor or less. The ether microcontroller controller does not have the internal power register but most likely modern microcontroller we're happy. All right so let's say you were connected to it as no part resistor. This is a register connector outside the microcontroller that is connected to a height. Let's say a micro microcontroller is operated a tree by tree will you connect it to a tree by tree. Well all right this is trip retrieval. And then you have a register and then let's say if you're reading in your output register over here again if your reading is set to zero this most part will be turned off so these mosques also be bitten off. And then this time will be broken. And when the current flows here we can see that our energy is actually pulled up to the VTC by this sister by the nervous system. And then if the V is equal to one in the output that register is equal to 1 and then right now this thing is turned on when it's turned on the Charon is a this is connected around at least pain is connected well. So instead of Carol going this way the current right now flowing this way right. So right now it is off. So by using up what resistor we can actually manipulate just eight of them.

OUTPUT MODE PUSH PULL CONFIGURATION

So let's say if you set the microcontroller 15 as output over here this morning we put it at 1 1 And then right now a supplement with a maximum of 50 megahertz and over here this to be you set it as a general purpose elbow push pull. By putting this to be it becomes your. Yeah. Actually setting this small example up a push pull. So general purpose output push bool you can assume that 5 copy and make emission with. Oh yeah. So this is the output P of the microcontroller. And this is the logic signal that we set in the register of the microcontroller. You can set it at 0 right 0 to the register of the microcontroller that you become 0. You said you want to become one for right now let's say. So I explain about how much more so and more you can refer to this arrow if this voltage or if this voltage over here if this voltage over here is higher than this voltage over here and then this and most is this and most transistors are quanta. So you can assume that these emotions are going to be a straight line and this thing is actually connected with these so let's say if this being over here an internal signal is set to be 0 0. OK so this voltage over here and this mortgage over here is the same and it's not happening if the voltage over here is not higher and this is over here this and most transistors are not conductive. So you can assume that it is actually an open circuit that you can assume that it's an open secret and there's nothing over here. This being is not connected to this one though. So right now most transistor that's a view that they ping the signal right. So the voltage over here and this voltage over here is actually high. Are you suggesting the So for this P most transistors to be conducted rotationally. Yeah, it must be higher than this one. So when each one chances that it's not conducting it's not so open overhead Jillian open circuit in this thing over here is zero. And this being over here is higher than this pin. So right now the p most is actually connected. So this being BDD is booking the rotation and it's almost similar to this I mean these transits that any contact. So right now let's go back to what these beings say for the imbalance. Now you say neuro right you say a zero these and most this is actually not actually off. And then for these prices I think it is actually planned on.

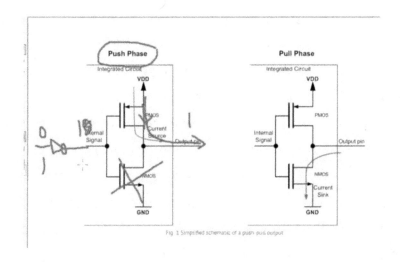

Fig. 1 Simplified schematic of a push-pull output

So right now this output would become high is actually for the current from BDD. You opposed the current good output. So that's why we call it horse face so usually because when you said he had zero and in APM become one word. Right. So maybe in time the internal microcontroller would not be great. All right. That would be not the when you say zero you become one. When you say as one it becomes zero. So right now E You said it as zero. So this is what we call it push rates decided as zero and then over here you could say yes 1 it become a cool phase we are in when you said 1 in the register microcontroller the output is in the pool phase because you say as one this and most transistor it's every turning on because when you say that's one right this voltage over here is actually higher and these more fish over here they transfer things turned on and these voltage over here is to similar to almost similar to these voltage over here. So they hold on and then this other thing it's actually pulled to the ground. So if there's any current flowing into this being the current it flows towards the ground. So the pool holds to the ground. Okay. And then push is current sourcing and then Paul pool is currently making So this is how Paul works in the microcontroller.

LED BLINKING

And I recommend you all to download a safe as a PDA so we can use it as a reference in the future. It is around one thousand and one hundred and thirty four pages so right now let's get started. So first order the bling the LAPD we need to do some GPA or initialization. So right now let's create a uh function which does the GBI or initialization GPI. Oh I mean me. I mean so this is the function and put a while loop inside the main function and then this GPA or initialization is we need to create a portal type function and then we won let's say you want to bleed out at a certain interval. So we create a delay. We have to create a delay. So which means that all Integers are equal to zero. I am smaller than a certain value, let's say five million.

This is four hundred five thousand five million. And then last plus I. All right. So which means that the delay these follow is the definition for the delay. So we can put a delay over here and then put all this over these nine days to the code that will bring that out and then right now let's try to compile it. So right now it is giving us a warning. It says that the eye is defining right now because in the previous year I didn't set the scene nine nine more in order to use a defined eye in a file that looked like this. We need to set scene nine. Ninety nine more. So let's go to flash. Go to configure flash to go to CC + +. Over here is the C ninety nine more. We need to enable it. That's And then let's try to compile it. Do it any more alright. And then right now what we need to do is we need to do the GPI or initialization OK so to initialize to to set up the GPI all we need to do is enable the clock for the GPA offers.

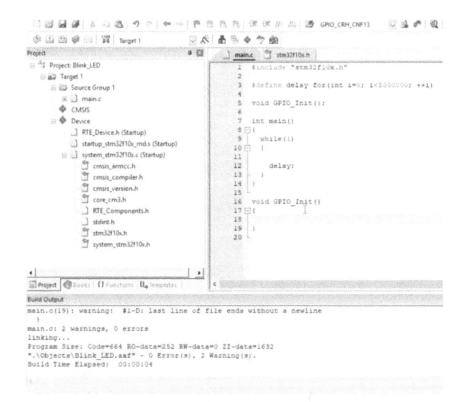

```
1    #include "stm32f10x.h"
2
3    #define delay for(int i=0; i<5000000; ++i)
4
5    void GPIO_Init();
6
7    int main()
8    {
9        while(1)
10       {
11
12           delay;
13       }
14   }
15
16   void GPIO_Init()
17   {
18
19   }
20
```

Build Output
```
main.c(19): warning:  #1-D: last line of file ends without a newline
   }
main.c: 2 warnings, 0 errors
linking...
Program Size: Code=664 RO-data=252 RW-data=0 ZI-data=1632
".\Objects\Blink_LED.axf" - 0 Error(s), 2 Warning(s).
Build Time Elapsed:  00:00:04
```

So in this go to the Ashley house is the intersection RCC we need to go to actually see the register that's in the register called APB to end our So in this register. You can see that. So right now we want to bring the LAPD which is located on the desert LAPD which is connected to the policy pin 13 of the microcontroller which is located on the block. So we'll be blinking the LAPD. So right now we want to enable the policy of the microcontroller or the input output in so we won't do anybody's this bit. All right. To enable this be so this be located and so I O P C enable.

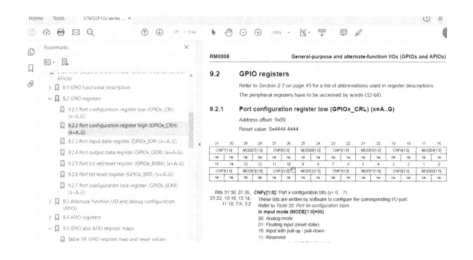

So we can see that this is a policy that enables you to enable the clock for the policy. So right now it is located in these tragedies that we're going to bring out the one right now. First we take out the RCC. This is the first tree. Correct the RCC. And then when you see this on this call it back it as the reference. So this is the reference we can see that the rest of the list of which register you want to reference. I would choose the APB to be an R okay. So this is and then you'll be all equal. We won before right. So we can actually go to this data file because there's already a beat definition for the instead of writing a to duplicate just write it as one sheet that is by far right. We can actually just do it this way but I prefer the destination for this hexadecimal value. So right now I can go to this data file I can search for RCC you can tackle it can press control and search for RCC and you will search for RCC for you my next findings. Okay go right RCC ways RCC All right. Somewhere over here RCC APB to the All right is uh is over here. So this is uh the definition for this hexadecimal value so I'll copy this one go to the main function meantime go to mean file right now replace it with a hacksaw and replace this sex this one. So this is how you enable crop Pol Pot seed All right. After that you enable the crop for policy you need to set it as output pin. You need to set that GPA. Oh let's go back to that. She closed this section. Go to the GBI. Oh right now I want to set the pot. Okay as output to set it as output. All right, let's go to this register. So far this register we have to register this to register GPA OCR hitch and GPA OCR app. So see our register is to do the configuration for pin 0 2 pin 7 you can see that this number 0 see an f 0 with this 4 B is a it represented as the configuration for the pin 0. This 4B is hoping one pin to pin tree and the pin 7. So right now we want to do the configuration for pin 13. We should go to see our page so see our hash is to do the configuration for pin a pin Kristie. Right now we just want to do a configuration for pin 13. So we just care about this for the twenty three to twenty. All right. So first we want to set it as output mode. Max speed 50 megahertz so this should be 1 1. All right. It's two to one and one and then twenty three and twenty two we want to say as general purpose output push pull zero and zero. So it will be 0 0 1 1. This is what we want. All right but you can see that the initial reset value is 0 x 4 4 4 4. So 4 is 0 1. So far it is 0 1 0 0 so go back to the. You can see that this hex value is 4. So it would be 0 1 0 0. So right now it is 0 0. You want to set it as 1 1. Let's go back to the code we can back GP I see just now. I say that in order to set the value for the register first we look at the first the corrective behind on this call. So with that GPI 0 GBI 0 and then the X is represented X is equal to it can be categorized into two G. It can be a b c. So right now we want to bring the LCD a policy in 13 so GPA is the ICC and then add the underscore over here. That's Angus calling with that reference. See our hitch. This is the register that runs the orange register. So you'll be all equal or equal. So instead of having the hexadecimal value I can beat the destination. Let's go back to the GBI or see you somewhere around here. GP I always see our hitch mode 13. This is why I want to go to mode 13. This one. So this one is 0 0 23 which means that over here is 23 so a bit equal to this one. So right now let's go back to it. We have twenty three twenty two twenty one and twenty the initial value. The moment that you reset it is equal to 0 1 0 0. Right after that you want to set the model. This to be is the most B you want to say yes 1 1 and then right now we all we all do it a bit. Operator we 0 0 1 1. All right. So right now the value in the register. See our highest register is 0 1 1 1. So is being set into optimal already so you queue this line of code. So right now we want that GPI O C we want to set it so we want to clear this being we want. We want it to be the general purpose of our book Push pull. Okay so these two pins equal zero and zero. But right now the value is 0 1. We want to set it back to 0 0. So to set it back to 0 0 GPA OCR age this all and equal to not GPA. Oh see our hitch. CNN 13 OK so this GPA OCR H student F 13 we can see that is represented as 0 0 C.. All right. So e c c c is equal c is equal to Uh 1 1 0 0 in binary so if you're invested right now you can see that in our quote right. We do the inverse of the value. So right now it will be equal to when you inverse c you'll be equal to 0 0 1 1 and then we do. And or we use and operate the we multiply the register with the using and operating with this one. Let's go back to playing Let's go back to this one. We do it and operate that multiplication. We do that and operator and we've uh 0 0 1 1 So right now the value will be 0 0 1 1. Okay. So this 4B right now would be equal to 0 0 1 1 general purpose of a push pull and output note Max be 50 megahertz. So notice that when you set the mode into output mode you follow everything every bit that the bit that you set in the CnF register. SB It will fall into this region. If we studied as input you fall into this region right. So right now we have configured it. We have the GBI all initialization that's called the GBI or initialization function. So right now we want to bring that out. I would like GBI O C or is this all equal. JP I O paying 13 so right now this debate is open that it is not defined. I would create a new group. So this is a new photo uh I would name it s user libraries my library is and then I create the two files I create will first create a GBI all files out your name. You bet. How do you buy it?

```
_| man.c_  _| stm32f10x.h
  1    #include "stm32f10x.h"
  2
  3    #define delay for(int i=0; i<5000000; ++i)
  4
  5    void GPIO_Init();
  6
  7    int main()
  8  ⊟{
  9        GPIO_Init();
 10
 11        while(1)
 12  ⊟    {
X  13          GPIOC->ODR ^= GPIO_PIN_13;
 14          delay;
 15  ├    }
 16  ├  }
 17  ┘
 18    void GPIO_Init()
 19  ⊟{
 20        RCC->APB2ENR |= RCC_APB2ENR_IOPCEN; // Enable clock for PORT C
 21
 22        GPIOC->CRH |= GPIO_CRH_MODE13;
 23        GPIOC->CRH &= ~(GPIO_CRH_CNF13);
 24  }
```

Oh. Edit I created us uh uh uh maybe I used it was great out here so here's the CFL so I only be using the how'd you get what I paid for. So in the file I would find all the I would define the definition for each pin. So four pin zero is you. 0 0 0 1. So let's say let's go to the GPL or the. Right. So this GPL or the register when you set it lets say a pin. Uh. Yes. After you have done the configuration for pin 0. Right. So if you set it as one over here the pin 0 will be high. So let's say if it sets the axes a. So right now GPA or a pin 0 would be high. So if so it is 0 0. If you say yes 1 you would be one if the pin would be high value added to you then it would be high. So right now we wonder if we want pot seeping 13 so. Okay so let's do this one US GPI open zero. So let's say if you want it to be high you just put instead of putting it off you put the hexadecimal value 0 1 become one you put GPA or pin 0 to replace the hexadecimal so we can remember it is the pin 0 all right. So I want to pin treaties and definitions. I will be using this definition. So we won't pin 13 right. So this printing will be copied over here. So in order to use it I have to include the hate file that I've just created. How GPA Oh Dot hitch a default. All right you can see that there's no red light anymore. And then so. Oh yeah we can see that GP I O C or the out initially the value is 0. So this is all operator. This is a resort operator okay. This operator the function is to the moment let's say I have a and b value say 0 0 0 1 1 0 1 1 and then go to a or b when you have one you be equal to 1 when that's when you only have 1 1 you'll be a good 1 that's 2 1. If the value a and b is equivalent becomes zero if a and b is different I would become one. Okay. So right now in your GPA Oh c o The outright so this you better see Odie out initially. Is it good with 0 0 0 right now? Because I saw a. Go back to GPA. Oh. I saw it GPA open 13 so GPA open that it is your x 2 0 0 0 so initially is Georgia 0 0. So I saw it with your X 2 0 0 0. So when I saw it with 2 0 0 0 it would be equal to zero. X 2 0 0 0. Okay. After that the moment when you execute this code initiate initially the value is low for being 13 right now after you saw it with your X 2 0 0 0 you'll be Koto 2 0 0 0 2 2 0 0 0 x 2 0 0 0 is equal to 0 0 1 0 0 0 0 0 0

0 0 0 0 0 0 0 0 0. Okay so this is pin 13 over here. Kim 13. So right now pin 13 is going to 1 asked to you as a gift. This line of code pin 13 goes to 1 from 0. It goes to 1 right now. The LTTE will become bright and then you go to delay after you've finished a delay. You go back to the base when you execute this line of code right now. See the will. The value is your x 2 0 0.

$$G\ PIOC \rightarrow ODR = 0 \times 0\, 0\, 0\, 0$$
$$| \quad 0 \times 2\, 0\, 0\, 0$$
$$\overline{\qquad 0 \times 2\, 0\, 0\, 0}$$

$$0 \times 2\, 0\, 0\, 0 = 0\, 0\, 1\, 0 \quad 0\, 0\, 0\, 0 \quad 0\, 0\, 0\, 0 \quad 0\, 0\, 0\, 0$$

As you saw it with your X 2 0 0 0 right now because of 0 1 0 0 saw 0 0 1 0 0 it will be equal to 0 0 0 0. So right now 0 x 0 0 0 0 0 0 bad output. Okay because when you are an equal villain you become zero and it's different. Over here. Is different when you become one. So right now you execute after the delay you execute that like the code again the pin 30 over here in all the entities you become zero so it becomes high after DeLay becomes law after DeLay becomes high again after DeLay becomes law again and then you blink at a certain interval. So right now we compile a file using a code to the microcontroller.

ON BOARD LED HIGH LOW INVERTED EXPLANATION

So this the idea that we are going to toggle it to make it high and to make it low and is actually connected to the pin cutting do you get see me for my sister. So right now I will show you all how to toggle on board our eating so go to the idea and I read in the code what you need just as you get initialization. So in this GBR all initialization I have enabled a crop for the plot C because we are going to use policy and then these two lines of code is to configure the king 13 seeking 13 to be a push pull mode output push pull mode. So I've thought about it in my blink PBS video. So right now I can be called and go to Daddy's back session and then do. First you need to run the code and then go to the peripherals system the GPI oh gee Can't you see though this in the property.

These are the registers that belong to Jabbar Ozy. You can use it to turn on the pin and turn off the pin by going to. Yes. Ah. So let's say you want to turn on the Dubai or see pin 13. You can click on the beat as 13 and if you want to turn off the pin 13 you can actually click on the be our tag team be our which means that we said and B S E B said so you can click on it. Right. So this is the S R register to know that I should add these pin 13 be set pin 13 and be reset pin 13 so and you notice that if you click on the B S 13 right you set it right. The LGB on your microcontroller on your entry to board your turn off. If you click on Big B set out of your microcontroller you turn on and work but actually it is purposely designed in this way. And we call it our current thinking method. Right. So this is how the EDI is connected. We have a register with a microcontroller. So in this box is actually the internal structure of the microcontroller. So you see that I have configured my microcontroller in output push pull mode so you can go to configuration. So this is the output driver. It has the most transistors and most transistors I have drawn in here. So it says that if you are configured in push output push pull mode. When you set a zero let's say you set a zero in your BSR register right in your upper register right. When you set a zero you actually activate the most. So when you give it to an MOS you're actually driving and turning on the TV on the microcontroller. So the current right now caps rose from tree by tree and most go to the animals and then go to the ground gradually sinking the current. And how it turns on. Right. So if you set one in your output that is just then what happened. You set one. You actually activate the chemos so you just negate the end loss activating PMO. So right now this is high.

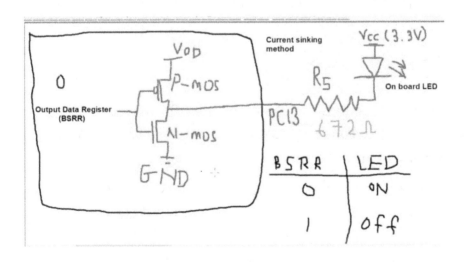

And then there's no particular difference between these P.S. 13 and the BBC. So right now it depends. So is the reason why I say just now when you set zero in your upper register. Yes. Are the LCD turned on and you set one in your bed as are the LCD tens of. And the reason we are designing it in this way is because the internal structure of the microcontroller is not designed to source more current and sinking current because they are able to see more current and source Kyra right. Maybe you might think that why don't you design this way because if they design this way they say you'll be setting a zero at the end Mosley's turning on the most is turning on and then you put the ground. It works. But let's say if you say S1 the end was the most tense of the pin was turned on and then right now the associated carbon but the current source. Right. And then by the internal structure of the microcontroller maybe it's just very little compared to the current that can be sourced by a cheap retrieval power source. So maybe it's just let's say 10 million. Right. And then right now it even goes to full brightness maybe only goes to have brightness and is not what we won. You won. We won. We need either to go into full brightness or fully turn off. Right. If you are using a Palestinian method. Yeah. Able to sing a lot. Because the carrot is actually provided by the tree well. So in this case it's actually a power source that comes from the USP. So maybe you can go up to a hundred million. Right. Right now the rest is used to meet the current. So the rest is done which is label as RFI You can see that over here on the backside of all as the interview microcontroller is the high register you can measure the rest is then of your rest is on your microcontroller board maybe it comes from a different vendor you're less than that you would be different. And I mean you can actually calculate how much carbon actually uses my day on what EDI and when it goes do I go to find a schematic on Google. So is reading five hundred and ten ohm but what I measure is and two imagine yourself.

UART FRAME STRUCTURE EXPLANATION

We have to stop B and Stop B and also in the lingo you frame why they only had a bit of dot that you did. Why don't they put sixteen bits of data or Danny phobia of data or even a little bit of data right. And I'm going to explain about it in my drawing over here. So let's say right now when I configured the speed after sending the back out right at one beat per second. So for every second I would send out one bit at a transmitter site and the receivers I also configure it to read the data which is sent by the transmitter at the speed of one bit per second as well. But right now the problem is when I configure both sides in standing and reading it that I read or speak of one beat per second. The problem is that I'm not going to have the exact same speed in sending and receiving. So maybe there will be some small errors in the speed of communication. They say the sender sent one beat per second but actually if in reality the receiver recent data like it one bit. Everyone plays for one second so there will never be this kind of small error. A rise in ready D. Right. And this is a big problem when you do not have a stop stop because he is not going to provide synchronization.

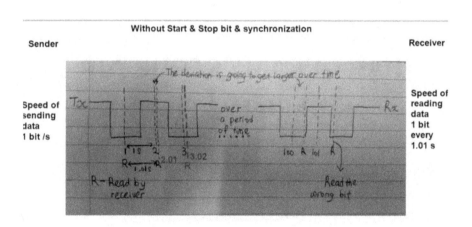

So let's say right now we're and he's actually sending out a top right for every one second. So we hear one missed that one second to wish me a safe second So at the first second right now actually sending out an attacker at a meter of this be the receiver reached the top. And receive a reason data over here and then after that after one in either one second to second. Right now the sender sends out that adapter. OK but right now the receiver is going to read the dagger and beat everyone by July 2nd. So the receiver you read the data 2.0 one second right now. So right now you can see that there's a deviation surprisingly from the receiver's recent data to second but right now it reads the dagger 2.0. One second. All right. Now add a second that the sender sends out a dagger again like right now the receiver's recent data entry points to a second. So we can see that the deviation is going to get larger and larger and before that is division is your boys your 1 second in reading in the delay of reading right. And then the second that erases your points, your second in a delay of reading. So let's say when it comes to over a long period of time I did 100 seconds supposing the recent data was 100 seconds right. Right now it reads the data at this point. At this point and then at 100 hundred one second. It should read this bit of data but right now it reached the wrong beat attacker. So it gives us the wrong gathering. So it means that the dust that is spotted by the deviation is going to get larger and larger over time and it reaches the wrong data and it gives us the wrong information. So how to solve this problem. So let's see right now we have stopped beating you up. All right. So this is a song you offer him over here. So let's say right now at the start BRand transmitter sent out a darker the receiver read the data. Okay. And at the second B the transmitter sends up the dot dot again. So there will be some small delay in reading the data. ABC up 1 0 0 0 1 second but right away it comes to that. It beats the seven beats it beats right in reading and a deviation is going to get a little bit larger than the first beat but right now the good thing is the deviation is going to stop here. So he's going to stop it and it's not big here. And then at this start of a new frame the receiver knows that he's going to start reading again and that ego is going to read the data and for the first beat that would be a big issue it's going to start from small again and then division right now will slowly increase and due to a bit and it will start all over again. So which means that right now the deviation is just going to even grow. But you grow argue that it beat and then it will stop and then right now at a new you out frame is going to start again and then it will stop and it be and this is also the reason why a single you out frame they only have it be because they don't want to allow the deviation the delay of reading the data gets larger and larger. So just imagine when you're a single you out frame right you have 32 bits of data when the reading of data minor deviation gets larger and larger. Right. Maybe at the last bit editors did do a bit of data there might be a chance that he's going to be wrong. So that's why they just restrict the size of that bar in your frame and make it only a beta right now. I guess you already understand why in a single you out frame we have a start beat and they stop beat. This is to prevent the delay of reading the data gets larger and larger and they also restrict the size of the data in a single you offering.

BAUD RATE EXPLANATION

I explain about race or about the communications between your sender and your receiver using your communication. So over here in the dark I shit in this fashion about regeneration. This one is the formula that you use to calculate the use at the Ivy. Based on the rate and input call to the peripheral. So this right over here is about the rate that you won for your communication. So the most commonly used bar rate is 9600. So if you won your communication speed to be 9600 you just said it would be 9600 over here and for the SDK is the input to the peripheral. So depending on your user that you're using. So if you are using that one then your input cost is different. However if you're using two , three , four or five then your input costs are different. So how can you know what is the input crop with a peripheral that you are using. So you can come over here. This one in the memory bank and architecture so you can see that for use that one they are using an APB to back or use at two three four or five guys using an APB one. So these two bus they have one difference so we can come to this site you can see that it says that the APB one bus is limited to 36 make an APB to bus is operated at full speed 70 up to seven to make I heard it so sees my frequency is seven to eight megahertz.

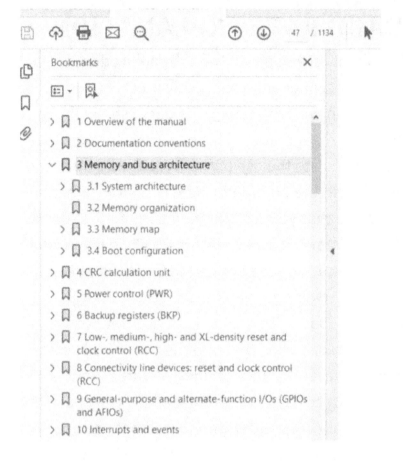

These are interconnected using a multilayer AHB bus architecture as shown in Figure 1.

Figure 1. System architecture (low-, medium-, XL-density devices)

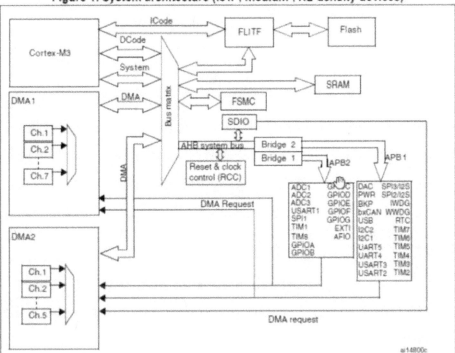

So my you at one will be operated at 72 mega has an APB to a bus. Right. You can see over here at one APB to the bus. All right APB to bus. Okay let's go back to the current generation. So since you're a note input implicated Perry Farrell 72 megahertz and about rate 9600 you can calculate their use at the Ivy. So once you calculated the use at the Ivy you can use your use at the Ivy to calculate your use that be our value. So once you've got your use that to be our value you can go to the user register use at the register you just put your use that be our value into this register. All right. After you put your value in in this use that be our register then you're about to be configured with a battery that you have set in the formula just now. So yes you have said 9600 right now about race 9600 right. And then. All right, let's go back to this one. So this is number one they are using the reverse calculation you are doing reverse calculation. They already have to use that to be our value and then we calculate it use at the IP value is not what we are going to do. We go to example 2 and then so let's say it depends on your input to the peripheral and about the rate that you won. So let's say right now I calculate that my use at the Ivy is twenty five point six to first. I need to separate it into the fraction and month side so Mandisa is the integer value of your use at the Ivy. So integer value has no decimal. Right now your use at the Ivy is twenty five point six to your integer value should be decimal twenty five and then you need to convert it into hex ivory which is 0 x 1 9. And then as for the fraction you get the decimal value the decimal value of the use at the Ivy is zero point six two. And then you need to multiply it by sixteen.

Example 2:

To program USARTDIV = 0d25.62

This leads to:

DIV_Fraction = 16*0d0.62 = 0d9.92

The nearest real number is 0⍟10 = 0xA

DIV_Mantissa = mantissa (0d25.620) = 0d25 = 0x19

Then, USART_BRR = 0x19A hence USARTDIV = 0d25.625

Example 3:

To program USARTDIV = 0d50.99

This leads to:

DIV_Fraction = 16*0d0.99 = 0d15.84

The nearest real number is 0d16 = 0x10 => overflow of DIV_frac[3:0] => carry must b
added up to the mantissa

DIV_Mantissa = mantissa (0d50.990 + carry) = 0d51 = 0x33

Then, USART_BRR = 0x330 hence USARTDIV = 0d51.000

Table 103. Error calculation for programmed baud rates

This is the formula you have to follow. Right. And once you have multiplied sixteen you get a nine point ninety two. And then you need to find the nearest real number for nine point ninety two and then the real number is 10. And then you hope you have to convert it to somebody as well which is 0 say And then you have to add a Mandisa and a freshman using all operators. Once you add it up you get 0 x 1 9 8. All right. And then this is your x1. You can put into your use that be our register then you're about right you'll be configured. So this is an example too. Right now let's go to an example tree so let's say again depending on your coffee question your battery that you want. You can clearly use it at the Ivy. Right now your use at the Ivy is fifty point nine nine. First again we have to separate our impressions into monkeys. All right first we separate into function. OK so your decimal value is zero point nine nine. You have to multiply it by 16 which is fifteen point eight four. And then for your fraction value it cannot be more than 16 the largest correction well you can only be 15. So since right now your fresh is fifteen point eight for every convert it into a real number. Right. Sixteen is sixteen which is overflowing already. OK because your freshman value only occupied the first 4B. OK the first ball bit which means that the value can range from zero to 15 only. But right now your value is sixteen okay. When you convert it into room number 16. So it's all low. And then once it's overflowed you make sure the carry is added to Mount Isa. And so I get my keys outside you have to add one so right now let's say you decide because you monetize the integer value which is 50 so 50 head has to add one and in the count 51. OK so 51 when you convert into hex it is your ex that is the tree right now because of your friction already the overflow of your friction is added to Mount Isa. Right now the fraction will become zero then you use that out. It will be a mantis area at your fraction using the all operator which is your ex that is the tree plus the fraction

0. So what you get is the Zero X tree tree. Zero. So this is your ex Treasury zero you then go into your use that we are registered. All right. So this is how you continue about the rate using this formula by calculating the use at the Ivy and then convert it into use to be our value. Okay. Thank you so much for watching.

PARITY CONTROL EXPLANATION

I will talk about charity control. So clarity control is actually a mechanism used by you to check whether this area in the truck has a transmitter. So at a receiver site you use a parody control mechanism to check whether your data is corrupted. Right. So apparently control can be separated in two even parity mechanisms or parity mechanisms. Let's play more about it later. So when you come to this control controlling the entire year you can see that it seems that the party control can be enabled by setting the PCAOB in the user control one register. So when you come to this user register as a user see I want you click on it. And then there's a PCAOB in the PSB. So for the PCAOB is used to enable the parody control and then for the PSP is used to select the rider you want it to be even parity or parody. All right. So by default 0 0 0 0 in this register so which means that apparently control is desirable and even parities every selector even is quasi configured to even parody stick and use it because the parent controls disable. So right now.

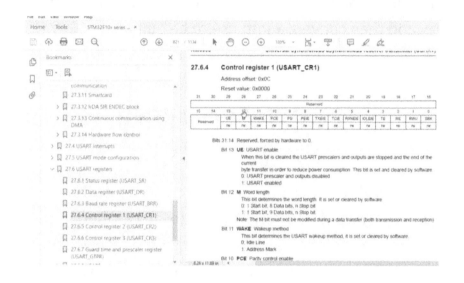

And as a negative call and B. So this B is to determine the data that you are going to transfer. So it is set to zero or be it that orbits and it is set to 1 and is night out of. So this data to enable the parody control that it cannot be even include the parody if you say tonight Stop it. So if you put it the one at the end B oh here the first it will be your daughter and the last B will be Perry DP. All right. So let's go back to parody control. So this frame format depends on your and B or your PCAOB. What is being said in both of these B right. Let's go through it. So if you set your NBA X to zero value which means that the number that you want to be so it is a bit in the parity Control B zero. There's no parity B all right. So for the second one if the NBA is good, the total number that they want to transmit is eight B but the view that I give you that is going to transmit to the register is just seven B and the last bit is the parity. Right the parity occupies that last bit. So let's go to 90. So for the NBA when you set it 1 it means that the total number of data transmit is Niobe without a parity b the PCAOB is set to zero and the last one is that if you said and b to 1 and the PCAOB to be white as well the total number of that either is going to transmit is 90 like the last bit is occupied by the Harry DP and your data is going to be just a B. So because usually we are transmitting hex value or correct their value. So our data is usually up. Right. So if you want to enable a parity control usually you have to enable the and b as well. Right. So that the number of data that you're transmitting a b and that you matter B which is a parity. All right. So for parity control. Right. So for this as B is agility we can hear the SB is that B. So for every use of that frame you would have a stop between a stop B. Right. So for next one perigee control it can be configured as even parity or parody. So I have written over here. So let's say if you want if your initial data is used you're 0 0 0 0 0 0 and then you configure your mechanism to be even parity. Right now your microcontroller calculates the number of one in your initial data. And then if you at 0 0 1 as your parity B to make the number of 1 in your data to be even right. So let's say your image that there's no one inside which means that a number or a mouth that number of one in your data is even a radio because even in 0 2 4 or 6 So that's why right now you're even parity you're parity. When you configure it into an even parity mechanism parity. It would be zero and then this is the data that is going to transfer you beat that either you want to transfer your initial data and your parity bill is going to be zero.

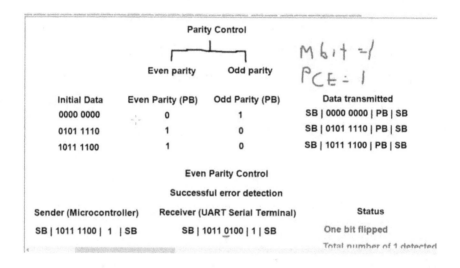

So if you configure your parity control mechanism to be on parity and you calculate the number of one in your initial data and to make the number of one in your data to be So you eat right now you ensure that that is 0 0 0 0 0 and then since there is no one you add a 1 to be the parity B all right let's go to a second one. So let's say right now this is your daughter. No 1 in your data right now is five. Right. Number one your daughter right now is five. OK and then for an even parody mechanism you calculate number one and make it even so season number one is five. You add another one so that a total number of one right now is six. You even and then for parity she's the number one right now already. You will not add one to your daughter. Instead you add a zero and then for the third one I see your initial that is this one. The total number one in your daughter is five. So to make it even number one you add another one. Do you hold to your initial data so that add to the number one right now six which is even so far the parity mechanism is the number of one in your data is five. So it is already all and then even add a zero as a parity. Okay. So since this one the total number of data that you want to transmit. Which includes your initial data and the parity. So you need to configure that and B to become one and PCV become one as well in your control one register. Just now I've shown you right in your control one or just the. This is your PCAOB and your and b you can. We need to write to become one. So I spend more detail about even parity control and how it detects the error when you're sending that to the receiver. So let's say your microcontroller side is your sender and your initial data. You want to transmit this one and this is your parity. All right. So because you're using an even parity mechanism it calculates the total number of one in your data. And so there are 5 1 in your data right now. You add another one to make it even number one in your whole data. Right. So right now let's say the moment that is transmitting to the receiver. So that's a big change over here right now initially it's 1. And then there's a big change to become zero. She's uh. So at the receiver's site one thing to note is that the receiver side sees you have configured your microcontroller set right to have an even Parry key mechanism so add your receiver side. So I'm using the access part which is a secret. I mean no. And my computer. So over here at a configuration you have to set a parry to be even as well. So Bozer has to be told the even parity mechanism and these are your receivers if you have configured it to be an even parity mechanism. Right. So you check for the total number of one in your data. So it calculates one two three four five. So right now there are a total of five in your whole data and you have configured it to be an even parity mechanism. So which means that there is something wrong which means that there is a change in the being of your data and one bit has lead. So right now the error is detected and then maybe even just this kind of data or maybe even request your microcontroller to send the data once again to the parents . How you configure it depends on the mechanism inside a microcontroller how to communicate. All right.

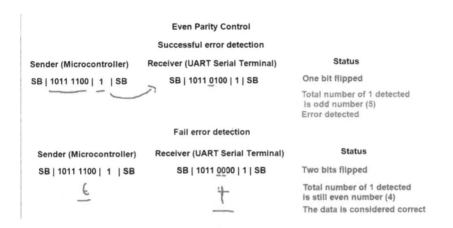

Even Parity Control

Successful error detection

Sender (Microcontroller)	Receiver (UART Serial Terminal)	Status
SB | 1011 1100 | 1 | SB	SB | 1011 0100 | 1 | SB	One bit flipped
		Total number of 1 detected is odd number (5) Error detected

Fail error detection

Sender (Microcontroller)	Receiver (UART Serial Terminal)	Status
SB | 1011 1100 | 1 | SB	SB | 1011 0000 | 1 | SB	Two bits flipped
		Total number of 1 detected is still even number (4) The data is considered correct

So this is a case where you successfully detected the error using an even parity mechanism. So in some cases your Eggo receivers that you also have you also failed to detect the error. So let's say your microcontroller side you are sending this whole data. All right. So they are using an even parity mechanism. So they are one, two , three , four , five , six. They are six number one in your data and add your receiver side. There are to be clips OK and the receivers I use that even have a parity mechanism. So right now you calculate the total number one in your whole data right now go to the number one and your data is four. And then just now it is C.. So six is even, four is even as well. And then it will consider the data to be correct but the actual data is wrong. So in this case it fails to detect the error in your data. And this is the advantage of the 3D control mechanism when you have one more than one big leap. All right. So the austerity control mechanism is still the same. If you calculate the total number one in your data. So it is you and your receivers. Me if he's still on then is correct it is even number one is not.

TRANSMITTING AND RECEIVING DATA USING UART IN KEIL

And this the code that I've written you can copy that scroll down slowly. This is a user initialization and GPA or initialization delay millisecond function and assistant handler. All right. And I read into code right now. Session so in this deposition I can see the data that I'll be receiving. So right now I run the code and this is the year to me now that I'll be using color SAS Part 3. You can download it just as a spot on Google then you can find it. And right now I can go to the configuration to set the rate that I want. So the rate in my code I've said it when I got in 600.

So over here I can set it to nine thousand six hundred as
well. So the bar rate needs to be seen at the transmitter
and receiver site and the zero part is console press. So
right now this is this. You can press it to fish on this fish of
the serial communication. So for every two seconds I
receive a halo from the empty too. So in this while you
can see that in this world. This fall I will be sending a data
stream so this string Hello from the entity to four if a
delay of two seconds. Right now you can see these ten
variables and I put them in the wash window. Right now
the value is 0 0 and is used to receive the data from the
computer. Right now I can say if I send one this is the best

I can send a data I put a one here I've been addressing. So this is the string that I received when I sent that out from the computer to the entity to receive a call from standard to reshape on an honest man. And then you can see that right now the time you received the correct one. So when I change it to when I send it again I receive a call from a standard to it right now. I received two. All right. So this is how it works right now. Explain more details about the code so these are to hate the fact that we need and then this is about the rate it wishes it would present 9600 and these are the global variables. We have a string and a string too. And this is the land beside the land that used to get the land on the stream and then land to use to get the land from the stream to and east and as it is used for the delay function. And these are the function prototypes that define. So in the main function first I get the length of the string that I want to send from my as the entity to the computer and then I configured a system.

```
31
32   int main()
33 □ {
34       len = strlen(string);
35
36       SysTick_Config(SystemCoreClock/1000); // Configure SysTick to generate interrupt every millisecond
37
38       GPIO_Init();
39       USART1_Init();
40
41       while(1)
42 □     {
43           for(int counter = 0; counter < len ; ++counter)
44 □         {
45               USART1->DR = string[counter]; // Transmit data over TX pin by loading byte into USART1->DR
46               while((USART1->SR & USART_SR_TC) == 0); // Wait until transmission is complete
47           }
48           delayMs(2000);
49       }
50   }
51
52   void USART1_Init()
```

So every January and throughout every millisecond This is used for the delay function and then I configured a GPA 0 GPA 0 initialization. So in the GPO initialization right now I'm using a plot a such as the entry to FTB I so this is the heart that I have set up the P A night of the entry to transmit and p e n is to receive the transmit which is p a night of the s the entry to is connected to the receiver pane of the FDA P A 9 code R X of the I and then P E can receive pain can I go to X of the s t the actor you should have disconnect on your side. So right now I am using only pot eight nine ten I would need to enable the club. This one is a clock for the input output, a GPA okay and then this is the alternate function put output because you are using an alternate function. I know that the pin at night and pin AT & TI use for alternate function instead of using it as a normal GPI opening. So I also need to enable the clock for the out of any function and then I need to enable that in a 9 4 to transmit pain so let's go to the GPI 0 0 register so right now we are just making 9 right. So is just this 4B 7 6 5 4 so I have drawn it here. So these are the four B that we are going to talk about and first you can see that the moment when the value is reset it is you ex fa fa fa fa so this four initially the hex that value is Fa So right now I need to configure D4 be in to out any function output push to an output not so issue 1 0 1 1 1 0 1 1 so initial value is 0 1 0 0 I run this line of code so you want to see what is this one you came by play go to destination and is actually retrieve 0 and then create 0 which means that tree trees actually equal to 0 0 1 1.

	7	6	5	4	hexa
Initial value	0	1	0	0	4
GPIOA->CRH |= GPIO_CRH_MODE9 | GPIO_CRH_CNF9_1;	1	1	1	1	F
GPIOA->CRH &= ~(GPIO_CRH_CNF9_0);	1	0	1	1	B

Baud rate = 9600

So right now this is a tree and then or this one where you go to your destination you can see that it's actually a right. So it is actually equal to 1 0 0 0. So this is the. Right. So right now it turns out that I added up you become 1 1 1 1 and then I run this call. I run this 9 if you're turning to this one be OK so right now this do I configure it into output mount an alternate function above push pull. So far the received ping you don't have to configure because we need to be input mode. And through the input the value is all by default. And you don't have to configure it. And then this is what it should be about initialization to configure in a knight and a P 18 as the transmit and receive a pin. And then for the user initialization you need to go to. So this is that you set initialization so to use the user. You also need to enable the club for the user. And right now you can go to APB to do it. So this user can use that one copy to enable you to have this register to enable this bit and maybe this one. And right now I will explain about the formula to calculate the rate. First you need to calculate the use at the Ivy and then use the use at the Ivy. To find out what is the value to put into your use that be our register. So you go to the USP register. Why just get to be out. Is that our value you put in SATs and then about right? Because you go to the value that you said. This is the formula which is used to calculate the rate and SDK is the input crop to the character which I use. I can then add about the rate here or it is about whether you want. So in my case it's 9600. Right now you can use this to a value to calculate the use at the Ivy. So I have calculated it. So right now this is my system clock and about the rate which I used to calculate use at the Ivy. I know you use the Ivy value of four hundred and sixty eight point seven five. And then once you get the use at the Ivy you can separate into a Monte site infection. So right now the monthly SA value is a round down number of use at the Ivy. So the round number is four hundred and sixty eight in Hanks is zero as one before and for the fraction is the decimal multiply with sixteen right now is 12th which is equal to zero x zero C and then once you've got the monthly site and the fraction you just added up using the all operator and then this is what you've got zero x 1 before C.

Baud rate = 9600

Usart_Div = SystemCoreClock/(16.0*baud_rate)
= 72000000/(16*9600) = 468.75

Mantissa = 468 = 0x1D4   Fraction = 0.75 * 16 = 12 = 0x0C

USART_BRR = Mantissa + Fraction

USART_BRR = 0x1D4C

So using this as one day for C you can put into it a that B register right now you're about right for your theorem communication is being configured to 9600 and so I'll go through it one by one again you can see that initially I get a system clock and about rate which I have set 9600 to calculate the use at the Ivy and then the Mount Isa which is an unsigned integer e round our number on the use at the Ivy. So let's say your use at the Ivy is fifty point nine nine. Right now my monthly salary is fifty. And therefore the fraction which is an unsigned correct fraction will be equal to the use of the Ivy. I know that use at the Ivy let's say is go to fifty point nine nine and then you will minus the might decide the man decides to round our number which is fifty point nine nine minus fifty which is zero point nine I multiply with sixteen so again zero point nine nine multiply sixteen you get fifteen point eight. All right so for fifteen point eight four for this function f f i x r. This function is to round up or round down the number. So when the value is greater than zero point five you round up to 1 when the number is smaller than zero point five. You round down a number. So let's say right now the value is equal to fifteen point eight for the value that I calculate sixty point four over here and then I round up the number you'd be sixteen. So right now officially it's sixteen. So if the fraction is sixteen is greater than 15 affection which means that it overflows and then the carry says that a carry must be added to the monthly s. And right now my desire is added by one. Okay. And then right now it's sixteen this edit by one and because a fraction is sixteen when the pressure is greater than 15 which is sixteen we just ignore it because we just want no value the fiction value to be 15 or under 15 on the 0 x 1 0 0 0 0 right. So this is 16 and then I n with an operator 15 which is 0 0 1 1 1 1 the value that I get will be equal to 0 0 0 0 0. So I just know the fraction if the value of the fraction is greater than 50. So this fraction right now is you know and a month is I just not have said one and then you put into that use that be our register. So this is how you calculate the rate and using this formula you can just be fined about the rate as you like it. You can define as 1 1 5 2 0 0 or whatever number that you 1 instead of calculating and manually you write instead of covering manually and then put in the value you have formula is better that then you can change it easily in the future whatever about rate that you want and then right now I need to enable to use that one interrupt this use I interrupt is to ask go to the Seattle one use that register use that C are one register over here so is the R X and e i.e. which is a fifth of the control register 1. So when I enable this receipt in the wrap it means that whenever there's a receipt b r x and B whenever that's our eyes and a B in the status register is high but interrupt you generate will be generated. So this is the interrupt this use that one I argue handed out is a receive interrupt that never does a data and that comes into this. And right now I also need to enable the user 1 receiver and then the transmitter and I use that so you can look into it and go to a C I want register. This is the NSA to our Eby this is our a B and then this is a TB this is a TB and then you see this is that you anybody use it. All right. And also we need to enable the global interrupt just now we have already enabled the receiver on the right. Right. You also need to enable the interrupt for this thing to function using this line of code. All right. Let me finish the user initialization right now in the while loop. So for every two seconds if you sing a string history hello from esta entry to an evil sound bite by bite so just now I get the Lang of the string right the length of the handle from the entity to and then at the. I was sent by bye bye which means that the first bite is Hesh which is Hello I'll send a Hey. So the hash. Right now I will look into the user register and then I will wait for the transmission to be completed. You go to the status register and you can see that there's a TCB. It says that whenever the transmission is complete it says that whenever the transmission is complete this will be set. So you just need to keep on checking while as long as the transmission is not complete you stay in this while loop and then after that the counter increment by one and you just look the next by into the data register and then you will send it again. Okay. And then for receiving the data you can see that the moment when there are X and B is race it means that the data is ready to be read and then you get the length of the string and then you send it back to the zero time you know of the computer using this followed by byte again and then you just read the data so you can see that even if I send it that offers and then I just read about that and that there won't be any effect on the register because the transmit data register and read that I registered are actually different.

```
6      // Global variable
7      uint8_t temp;
8      char string[] = "Hello from STM32\n";
9      char string2[] = "Echo from STM32\n";
10     uint8_t len,len2;
11     uint32_t msTicks;
12
13     // Function prototype
14     void GPIO_Init();
15     void USART1_Init();
16     void delayMs(uint16_t ms);
17
18     void USART1_IRQHandler(void) // Receive 1 byte at a time
19   ⊟ {
20         if(USART1->SR & USART_SR_RXNE) // Only true when the data is ready to be read
21   ⊟     {
22             len2 = strlen(string2); // Get the length of string2 to be transmitted
23             for(int counter = 0; counter < len2 ; ++counter) // Transmit data byte by byte
24   ⊟         {
25                 USART1->DR = string2[counter]; // Transmit data over TX pin by loading byte into USART1->DR
26                 while((USART1->SR & USART_SR_TC) == 0); // Wait until transmission is complete
27             }
```

So even though the syntax right now if I see that use that one out and use it one day at your window the syntax is the same. So we can see that in the user dot diagram you can see that we see that register and they transmit that outraged is registered they are different. Yeah. There are different kinds of registers so there won't be any problem even if I read you really first. All right. First there won't be it won't affect the data today you read in the user that I just read that out just the so I think this is it. So. So to summarize this function is in drag function is to read the data from the when you receive the receipt pin and then in the mean in a while loop this is to transmit the data to me every two seconds.

SINGLE CHANNEL CONTINUOUS CONVERSION

I explain about the ABC of that MTV to which I used to read it and a lot of value for a potential meta. So I decided to have that connection that I have set out on my site. So you can see that. Been on the potential meet that is connected to a trip by travel and the top right here is connected to the ground. And as for the media you know the potential media is connected to that in a 7 which is the GPI opium of the east the entity built. So I'm going to set up a seven as an ABC read and a lot of value from the potential media. All right. So right now I have a quote that I've written to interface with a potential meet. So you just keep on reading and a lot of value from the potential meter and then convert it into digital value. And so I write now slowly scroll down to code and you're trying to copy it. So this one is the interrupt handler which interrupts the risk routine. So when an ICE has finished conversion you can do this in the wrap handler. All right. And then this one is the main function. I do the configuration over here. I slowly scroll down right and this is the delay millisecond which I use in a lot of my videos

For generating delay in milliseconds and easier assisting. And let me just interrupt that view. A generator. Everyone made a second all right. So I was speaking about a quote in the main function. So right now I have my potential and I am already connected to my identity too. And right now I believe the quote I've written so let's be back in session so I see that when I run you right. So this is the variable that you will reach the data of the potential meter pin a. So you can see that right now when I can. I'm turning my potential meter to the next value. So the max value is around four thousand ninety six because he's a. And the maximum decimal value thinking goes up to E. What does it in 96. And it's connected in a seven right now tree by tree well and it has a value of four thousand ninety six. So right now I turn back to zero. So it gives us a value around 10 then the. So you can see that a red keeps on changing because the result is quite good. That's why let's say you get some slight change you will teach. Just change to Emily Will. And then you will detect it and get the value will also change race. Right now go back to the court and try to understand how to actually get it running for this first line of code is the config. So it's actually used to generate an interrupt every millisecond. So what are humans? You have to put it this one and then for the name of the interrupt. This is the name of the interrupt system handler. So the name is Felix. You cannot change it to any one but this interrupt service routine. And this is the config function. I actually got it from the website Dempsey's call and it says that to configure the system to generate an interrupt every millisecond you're correct. Right.

Code Example

The code below shows the usage of the function SysTick_Config() with an LPC1700.

```
#include "LPC17xx.h"

volatile uint32_t msTicks = 0;        /* Variable to store millisecond ticks */

void SysTick_Handler(void) {          /* SysTick interrupt Handler. */
    msTicks++;                        /* See startup file startup_LPC17xx.s for SysTick vector */
}

int main (void) {
    uint32_t returnCode;

    returnCode = SysTick_Config(SystemCoreClock / 1000);   /* Configure SysTick to generate an interrupt every millisecond */

    if (returnCode != 0) {            /* Check return code for errors */
        // Error Handling
    }

    while(1);
}
```

Function Documentation

uint32_t SysTick_Config (uint32_t ticks)

Initialises and starts the System Tick Timer and its interrupt. After this call, the SysTick timer creates interrupts with the specified time in free running mode to generate periodical interrupts.

Now of course this is the name of the assisting handler. I get it from this. Yes it's called. Because I'm also using the software component services call right. And then for this one for the second level code. This one is to configure the ABC scalar an equal frequency must not exceed 14 megahertz of the frequency of my entry two bodies seventy two megahertz and coffee Quincy tapes that are provided to the ABC I agree. Definitely to megahertz but I cannot use 72 megahertz because of crop frequency of the ABC cannot see 40 megahertz so that's why I have to use a preschooler to a day by day by day which means that you screwed out a clock that you supplied to the ABC. So I get information from the data sheet so you can come over here in the ABC introduction. It says that the ATC input club must not see 14 megahertz right and then you can come over here in the memory and bus architecture. You can see that the ABC 1 is actually connected to the APB to back and I'm using a BBC One in Mr. Terrill and the APB to the boss. You can come over here and see that in this region the APB operates at full speed. OK so which means that my ABC one is actually operating at full speed but right now go back to the ABC. So it's not that you cannot actually find it megahertz, so that's why I'm using a preschooler. So I need to go to a CAGR register. I just uh is over here in the RTC register right. Chapter 8 CAGR. You can't just be scalar. What is it um. Right. Oh all right. At least one with 14. And a big 14 and 15 and be 14 you can go. You can configure it to be

15 and 14 so there's an error in the sheet. So according to the speed of your microcontroller. So you have to choose accordingly. Your preschooler right now might be seventy two megahertz I speak. Actually 14 megahertz. That's why I divide it by six. All right now I get out my God. Okay. And you can get this definition when you right click it and go to the destination. Over here is actually defined in this hate file. Put it over here. Okay.

```
19
20      SysTick_Config(SystemCoreClock/1000); // Configure SysTick to generate interrupt every millisecond
21
22      // ADC prescaler (Clock frequency must not exceed 14 MHz, 72/6=12 MHz)
23      RCC->CFGR |= RCC_CFGR_ADCPRE_DIV6;
24
25      // RCC clocks for ADC1
26      RCC->APB2ENR |= RCC_APB2ENR_ADC1EN;
27
28      // Configure GPIO pin 7 as input with pull up/ pull down
29      GPIOA->CRL |= GPIO_CRL_CNF7_1;
30      GPIOA->CRL &= ~(GPIO_CRL_CNF7_0);
31
32      // Interrupt is generated after end of conversion of ADC (EOC)
33      ADC1->CR1 |= ADC_CR1_EOCIE;
34
35      // Enable ADC1 and ADC2 global interrupt in NVIC
36      NVIC_EnableIRQ(ADC1_2_IRQn);
37
38      // Set the sampling rate 239.5 cycles
39      ADC1->SMPR2 |= ADC_SMPR2_SMP7;
40
41      // Set the number of ADC channel used
```

And then for this line of code this is to enable the clock for the ADC 1. So for every peripheral usually they need a clock to run it. Right. For example for AIS grassy for you aren't for XP I designed a peripheral. So all these other peripherals need a clock. Okay. And to enable the client you can come to WD APB to even register to come to this

Dabashi over here in Chapter 8. This APB to all register which is a peripheral cloth enable register which is registered to enable Compaq for the peripheral. So you can see that for that many beats and each of the bases they are assigned to a different kind of peripheral plays a little bit for DS use that one enabled to enable the crossover to use that one. So right now what we need is this beat ADC 1 enabled. All right. So this one is to enable the clock for ADC 1. All right. Midnight. And by writing this one we are actually. Let's go to the nation so you can see that it's 2 0 0 0 right. So that means that 2 0 0 is actually 0 0 1 0 0 0 0 0 0 0 0 0 which is peak night. All right. So this is benign. And then for these two these two are to enable and GBI open seven is a configured GBI or a pin server as an input. We put our register or put our register okay to configure the Japan O pin 7. You can come to us this evening and go to the Chapter 9 reissues. It has everything about GBI or go to the GBI or register in the Japan OCR. Over here. So this one the outer edges that can have pain from 0 to p. 7. So what we need is pins. So these are the 4B that we are going to configure. So initially the value is for Pixar. So initially so far right. So fall which means that is actually 0 1 0 0 so which means that this second bead is actually this bit 30 is 1. So right now what we are going to do is that what we won is 2 1 0 0 0. All right.

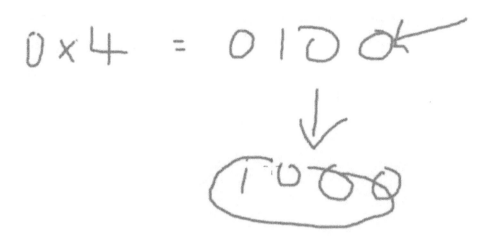

$$0 \times 4 = 0\ 1\ 0\ 0\ \text{ok}$$

$$\downarrow$$

$$\boxed{1\ 0\ 0\ 0}$$

So what we want is 1 0 0 0. So we go to combat this one.
All right. Okay. So this is what these two lines of code do.
All right. And then for this lie this one is to enable the
Interop interface to generate an interrupt bang. Yes. And
of conversion of the ABC. Okay. So this one is to tell you
tell us that the microcontroller that I want to generate an
interrupt. After the completion of ABC is finished. This is
in the control register so you can go to the ABC. ABC this
ABC go to the ABC register. So that's a control and control
register 1. So over here you can see that at 5 which is the
OCI. All right. This comes to this beat five. This one is to
generate an interrupt when the ECB is set. OK Ben. So this
ECB will be called Mendez. End of conversion of the ABC.
And after that if we enable these and interrupt will be
generated after the evil CBT says OK for this nine it says

that it will generate an indirect. All right. It just says that you will generate interest for this line to enable the global Interop You need to put this out of court in order to use it to interrupt this one . You just said that you were generating directly but it doesn't enable yet so to enable it you need to use this now. And this interrupt is this global interrupt. This is the interrupt service routine for the global interrupt. Even name it when that interrupt generates that you come to this interrupt service routine. So as for this line of code. So this one is to set the Central Time for the ABC. OK so central time is the time taken to read the data to the Senate. So go to that ice sheet in the Central Time register. This is a sample time registered to that I would be using sources I'll be using Channel 7 right. These are the Chibi that I'm going to use. So depending on your channel that you're using you have to set it accordingly. So even you said if you use channels you go sort of tribute 0 1 to ABC News Channel 1. These are a. There's a number followed by the S and P 0 to 9. In December I registered to. So if you are using Channel 10 and they're both in this other sample time register 1 they are going to use about a psycho if you set it to lower cycle by cycle then you get your data faster if you set it to higher cycle then you'll get your data slower because you will say to higher cycle time it takes the sample the attacker is longer okay and you you spend a lot time in sample the data and then you get your digital data slower and I have explained about the cycle the sample time in my another video so if you don't understand why it's this simple time I suggest you to go to Blue and to look about it in my other video so let's say right now I'm using a definition this one. So this definition excites me so it means that this tree is a tree one one one is two hundred thirty nine point five psycho. Okay but I want to show you all something. So let's say right now I said it to two hundred thirty nine point five Psycho which means that the time taken to sample that is the longest compared to other cycles. So right now when I built a quote and loaded you into my ball. So right now I rehab my ass two and potential meter to connect to my computer. And then I ran it when I saw this SDM studio and I'm going to use it. I'm going to use it to see any number of Central Data variables. Oh then wait, that's the variable number of central data. So it is over here. So I have created a number of simple data and every time when the indirect service routine for the ABC one is called and my desk data that is ready to be read the number of simple data is wearable will be increased by 1. Okay. And then these numbers of simple data wearable you are reset every one second. So this system handler you call every one millisecond ease and interrupt. So if the cow is increased to 1000 the number or of data is variable will be reset to zero. So you raise this wearable will be reset every one second and you see it in the end to do over here. All right. So right now when I run the code so you can see that for every one second and involve simple data that I get is

around forty five thousand forty four thousand. Okay.
Right now last.

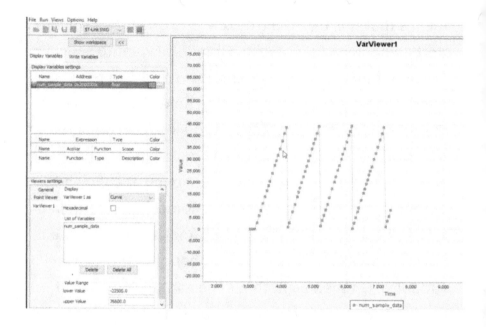

So actually I have created an excel sheet for the
calculation so you can see that when I rent a cycle it is
two hundred and thirty nine point five. Right. So I
calculated the number. This is the number of simple
seconds that I calculate is twenty seven thousand and just
now I measure it is around forty four to forty five
thousand. And this is the approximation 44000. So right
now let's see if I set a psycho to be one by five psycho

ways the number of said samples that we get per second. So let's go over here and I'm going to set it to zero so which means that this tribute is going to be zero. So each one by five psycho. So right now let's run it into the box and then we can see that right now I'm getting the data every one second I get around four hundred and twenty five thousand of data. So compared to just now the cycle is 210 units by five. The data that I get every second is just 40000. So it's ten times more when I set a psycho to be one by five psycho OK so these are the visa associates. So I have created the calculation for each of the cycles and then a number of samples. The second that I go I will get based on the cycle that I set to the best on the cycle that I set in the register. I will tell you all about what all this thing is about. So this is the ABC input clock. It is a child megahertz. They supply to the ABC 1 and this cycle is the cycle that is used to send both the analog voltage the lower the cycle the faster the sample time the higher the cycle the longer the sample time and for this total completion cycle. This one I calculate based on this formula. So that's a twelve point five cycle which is fixed. That's a useful conversion when you get there and a lot more dishes right. And then you want to do the accomplishment to digital that it takes chapter by five cycles and these are total conversion cycles. A chunk by five. Blast your cycle that you're setting the sample time register. And this is for the 2k column. This is total conversion time for one single data. So you said you calculate that based on the total commission cycle so right now the ABC is running a track mega. So this one is calculated based on the 14. The second is the number of psychos divided by the 12th megahertz. So this data means that the time taken is used to sample the data until it is ready to be read. So if you set a cycle to be one by five then the time taken to sample the data and get it ready to be released around 1 by 1 7 microsecond and then if you if the psycho is higher than the time taken to event you leave it at that that is going to be a lot longer compared with this one. Right. You can see that this rate of 5 microseconds is a lot longer. So for the fourth column this one is the number of samples that you get in one second is calculated based on one divided by this total conversion time. So it seems to get once in good data for this one right. Cycle one by five to get one single dot that it takes around one by one seven microseconds. So once again based on the calculation you get one hundred and fifty seven thousand from the doctor and this is a maximum of course. And of course theoretically you won't be getting this one because there might be some delay. Just now we have measured it right. You can see that when our number of Psycho is set one by five the number of samples that you get the second is four hundred thirty five thousand. By calculation. What we expect is eight hundred fifty seven thousand so maybe they say they asked for some delay in between and this is what you get in reality and therefore the two you can see that the number of samples the second decrease as the psycho increases. Right. So just now we have set the cycle to be two hundred thirty nine point five. While we calculate that is forty seven thousand but just now what we get is around forty four thousand forty five thousand in one second okay. And I have brought up the graph and this is a number of second samples that you get one second against the cycle that you set in the sample time register and think this is the most important thing that you've got to know. You can see that when you set the cycle to be longer and then you get a larger sample in one second. All right. So there is something not really accurate when we calculate what we calculate and what we get. So the error is quite huge when the cycle is set to 1 by five in the number of seconds that you get in the calculation and actually that you get. Right. But we do see that when the cycle is high the area is larger. So if you are designing ADC for the commercial purpose or anything then maybe you have to take everything like delay into account so that we can calculate the number of samples that you get in one second more accurately. Okay.

55.5	68	5.66667E-06	176471	142000
71.5	84	0.000007	142857	120000
239.5	252	0.000021	47619	44000

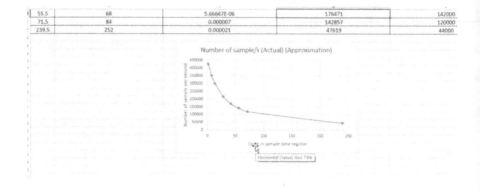
Number of sample/s (Actual) (Approximation)

So right now this line of code is to set the number of ABC channels that we are going to use. So since we are just using a Channel 7 4 to convert the no value to store value. So that number of ABC channels will be 1. And you can come to this ABC regular sequence one so you can see that for B twenty three to 20 is the B that we are going to set the number of channels that we are going to use. So you can see it's written as L which means the length of the channel. So by default the reset value of this register is zero. So this will be zero. So that's why we don't have to set anything. So you can see that you say that you reset to zero is just one conversion you'll be doing. So we just have one channel and then for this one this is only to set the channel in the sequence register. So this one is to actually arrange which channel that you are going to do the conversion first. And also since we are using just one

344

channel. Right. So we are just going to set the Channel Seven in sequence one. So these are the five that we are going to use for 2 0. So if you are one who says Channel Seven then I'm just going to put seven in these slightly number seven. So let's say right now if you are using two channels as you are using pins PIN 6 and pin 7 for ADC conversion. So you have a potential meter to read. So that's why you need to channel and then add the L over here. You are going to put two. So it's going to be one. Okay. And then in the sequence register you are going to arrange with the channel that you're going to do the conversion first. So let's say if you're using Channel 6 and Channel 7 you want to do Channel 7 conversion as they are going to put seven in this sequence. After that you want to do Channel 6 conversion and then you are going to put six in this sequence and do this five bit of the sequence. OK it's going to be seven in this guy and six in this five. All right. So again I'm going to explain this sequence is to allow for you to arrange which channel to do the conversion first and then this Lang is to set a number of channels that you are going to do the conversion. So it is a different thing. Right now he can see that since I'm using just Channel Seven right. So I'm going to set this 0 1 and 2 b to become 1 1 1. So it becomes seven. So you can see in my code the zero represented in the header file zero it represents 1 which is zero and then this one is represented bit one and then this one it represents two. All right. So a bit zero bit one bit too I said to one to represent Channel Six seven in the sequence one. OK so all right for this line of code the scan mode this can out. We are not going to use this in the third row. So I'm not going to explain it and therefore this one is to enable the ADC for the first time and set it to continue w mode. So for the ADC we need to turn it on two times before the conversion gets started. OK so we need to go to the control to register here. So it's a bit zero and bit one D on and continuous. We're going to go see what's inside and you can see that this zero is too kind on the ADC. So you can see that it says that if this b holds a value of 0 and a 1 is read and to eat then it wakes up the ADC from power down state. So it means that before this line of code was being used as a cue the ADC right now is in the power downstairs. And the moment when you set a bit to this beat, set a 1 2 this beat. He will wake up the ADC from the powerhouse stage. And then right now the conversion has not started yet. After that the conversions not only when this beat hosts a value of 1. Just now you have written one to eat right. So right now this bit holds a value of 1. And if you write a 1 to eat and a what. And if one is written to eat the conversion this time. So right now that's way over here. I said the A.D. I can turn on the ADC and then after that I delay one millisecond to turn on the ADC again. All right. So why do I delay one millisecond so you can see that it says that the application should allow a delay of the climb step so which is a time delay between the power up and tracks instead of conversion.

So over here this one is a power up and this one is the start of conversion. You turn on the second time it starts a conversion. So in between that should be a delay. So I just put one millisecond delay and you can play a role with it. I tried to set it into a microsecond delay to see what is the minimum delay that will get the ABC get started. Okay. So for this one is to set the ADC into continuous mode. So it means that the conversion will take place continuously. It will. It won't stop when you perform just one conversion. All right. And this is what we won. So right now after that I enable the calibration for the ADC after the power after I can on the ADC. Okay so I need to enable it. I need to put a delay before I do the calibration and because. So in this calibration section it says that before starting a calibration the ADC must have been in power and will stay for at least two ADC clock cycles. So over here once I can on the ADC the ADA on B is go to 1 After that I allow some delay before I do the calibration. Actually I'm not sure whether this delay millisecond is needed but just put it over here to allow the calibration so the calibration is actually used to reduce the accuracy error so that they would be more accurate. All right. So just putting a delay over here is just one minute one minute second delay so that maybe you can get a better accuracy for your ADC data. So the calibration B is set in the control register as well. You can come to us with this control register too. It's a bit too. So it's this that enables the calibration. So it seems that this be set by software to standard calibration and then after the calibration is done even reset automatically back to zero. So then after you enable the ADC calibration right you need to wait for the hardware. So you stay one as long as the calibration is not complete. After that you reset that hardware. And then this calibration bit you become zero. So this now of course is to wait for the calibration to be completed. So you should check for them. So it's a hacksaw value for. So which means that is actually beat too. So we check for B as long as it is equal to one. You stay in this while loop. And after that when the bit 4 turns into 0 and then you have the D while loop. So actually for this one you don't have to work this way. You can actually make it this way. So we will. Right to is the same logic as long as this B is good as long as the value that you get from the control register B is a good one and then we many. And we will be to as long as they are why did you stay in this while loop so after it turns zero and then the calibration is completed. You jumped out from this. Well. All right. And then next one is this interrupt handler. So this interrupt handler is the moment because you really need to enable it when that's the end of conversion right. So after the end of conversion you would jump into this interrupt handler and then you would check for the status register and then a competitor to UCB. So in the status register. Right. So that's the end of conversion be the moment conversion is a good one and then it emerges with this EOC. So this one the definition which beats one Yossi compared to this one after that once the conversion flat is said if you come into this over here you read the digital value from the data register and put into the above. So the moment you can see that you say this it is clear by the software or by reading the ADC the hour. Okay. So if you read the data from the data register this bit view actually being this bit The be in the the be in the status register you clear. So that lets say in case if next time you accidentally enter the ADC interrupts service routine again the B's are already clear and then you will not read the data again.

www.ingramcontent.com/pod-product-compliance
Lightning Source LLC
LaVergne TN
LVHW051429050326
832903LV00030BD/2984